Crawl Space Science

What to Have Done... *and Why*

LAWRENCE JANESKY

Crawl Space Science

What to Have Done... *and Why*

BY LAWRENCE JANESKY

Published by:

Basement Systems, Inc.
60 Silvermine Road, Seymour, CT 06483
800.640.1500 | 203.881.5090
www.BasementSystems.com

10th Edition

"Even at this early date, we calculate that we have saved our worldwide customers $32.8 million in natural gas, electricity and heating oil each year — forever, and ultimately many times more in rot repairs and mold remediation down the road."

— LAWRENCE JANESKY

THIS BOOK IS DEDICATED TO the the hard-working Basement Systems dealers and CleanSpace installers worldwide, who solve the mystery of how to create healthier, more energy-efficient environments for homeowners with crawl spaces every day.

Table of Contents

This is not a do-it-yourself book because crawl space repair is not a do-it-yourself job. It's hard work and takes specialized knowledge, skill and equipment. The purpose of this book is to provide enough knowledge to make an educated decision on what work needs to be done to your home, who should do it, and why.

Foreword

- A family in **Tennessee** has 37 floor joists replaced in their eight-year-old home.

- A **South Carolina** mother takes her four-year-old daughter to the doctor, again, desperately searching for a medical solution to the child's serious asthma and other symptoms.

- A **Connecticut** condominium board meets and the main topic of the discussion (again) is additional rot repairs needed. They approve yet another major expense — this time for $172,000 for the 36 units.

- An **Indiana** homeowner tries to lower his home energy costs, making frequent trips to the local hardware store for caulk, weather stripping, and insulation for his attic, all with little effect on his household fuel bills.

- An **Oregon** attorney writes a lawsuit for his client's mold claim, trying to include all the responsible parties.

- An **Arkansas** homeowner goes to work after making arrangements for someone to let the exterminator into the house to deal with the unwanted pest problem that he can never seem to get rid of.

- A **Virginia** family hires a firm to perform expensive mold remediation in their home and considers moving out until the work can be completed.

Why? Why is all this happening? Answer: dirt crawl spaces. There is no more serious and common defect in housing than vented dirt crawl spaces.

Old-Fashioned Ideas – Time for an Upgrade

There is no shred of evidence or science that says vented dirt crawl spaces make sense — and tons of evidence, right before our eyes, that says they are a serious problem. Yet over 250,000 new homes and thousands of additions are built each year with dirt crawl spaces. There are now 27 million of them. The building code not only allows dirt crawl spaces, but actually made the problem much worse by requiring them to be vented. Homeowners, and the U.S. economy, are paying the price in many ways. It's time for something to be done — right now.

Your home costs money to operate — to heat, cool and maintain. A vented dirt crawl space raises your heating and cooling cost by 15% to 25% every month, and makes it very likely you'll have a big expense for mold removal and/or rotted wood replacement (guaranteed in the Southeastern United States).

If it's worth owning a home with a dirt crawl space at all, it is certainly worth fixing...

CleanSpace®
Crawl Space Encapsulation System®

Your local authorized CleanSpace installer may have given you this book. If not, find your local CleanSpace installer by visiting www.DirtCrawlSpace.com.

1 MAIN FACILITY

2 JUNKLUGGER'S HEADQUARTERS AND SUPPLY WAREHOUSE

3 LOCAL SERVICES FACILITY

4 CONTRACTOR NATION TECHNICAL TRAINING CENTER

5 SPRAY FOAM, STRUCTURAL REPAIR, BASEMENT FINISHING

6 BROWN ROOFING HEADQUARTERS

7 MANUFACTURING AND QUALITY CONTROL CENTER

8 RESEARCH AND DEVELOPMENT

9 DEALER SUPPLY WAREHOUSE AND TRAINING CENTER

What do you want?

Take the Quiz

FINISH THE NEXT TWO THOUGHTS BY CHOOSING A, B, OR C.

I want...

A) Mold or rot.
You probably already have this, you can stop reading now.

B) Just a little mold and rot.
Then treat your crawl space with the wrong methods.

C) No mold or rot in my house
Then get it right the first time.

I want my monthly heating and cooling bills to be...

A) As high as possible without me realizing there is a problem.
You probably already have this, you can stop reading now.

B) A little lower, but I am still willing to pay more.
Then fix your crawl space halfway.

C) As low as reasonably possible!
Then have it fixed right. Don't take short cuts.

The premise of this book is that you want a mold and rot-free crawl space and energy bills as low as possible. Read on . . .

Crawl Space Terms of the Trade

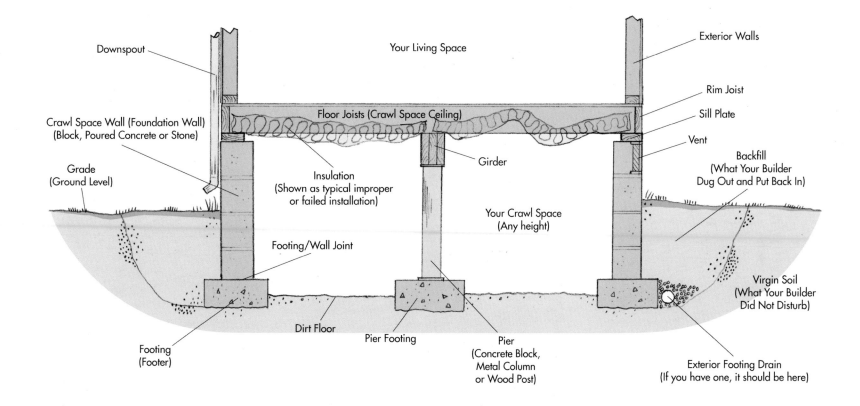

Downspout

Your Living Space

Exterior Walls

Rim Joist

Sill Plate

Crawl Space Wall (Foundation Wall)
(Block, Poured Concrete or Stone)

Floor Joists (Crawl Space Ceiling)

Vent

Backfill
(What Your Builder
Dug Out and Put Back In)

Girder

Grade
(Ground Level)

Insulation
(Shown as typical improper
or failed installation)

Your Crawl Space
(Any height)

Footing/Wall Joint

Virgin Soil
(What Your Builder
Did Not Disturb)

Dirt Floor

Footing
(Footer)

Pier Footing

Pier
(Concrete Block,
Metal Column
or Wood Post)

Exterior Footing Drain
(If you have one, it should be here)

CHAPTER ONE

WHAT LIES BENEATH

The Dirt Crawl Space Problem

Sure, you think: It's not very nice down there. It's cramped and uncomfortable and if you're not careful you are likely to whack your head on a pipe. It smells bad and it's dirty and buggy and damp. Sometimes it's just plain wet.

But... it's separated from the house! It's only a problem when you have to go down there to fix something. Right? Wrong...

The problem is moisture inside of a building, particularly because a building is made with organic materials, filled with objects made from organic materials, and lived in by people.

The moisture comes from two sources: **the ground and the outdoor air.**

Moisture from the Ground

On paper, in theory and in reality, exposed earth contributes a lot of water vapor into the crawl space air. The earth is damp, and as that damp soil dries beneath the house, the water vapor moves upward. In most climates where there are dirt crawl spaces, you can never dry the earth, and this invisible stream of water vapor from the exposed earth in a crawl space goes on forever.

There are several other ways water gets into a house. Groundwater seeps, leaks and even rushes into many crawl spaces. It enters under the footing, between the footing and the walls, right through block walls and through cracks in poured walls. After it seeps in, it just lies there in puddles, slowly evaporating upward into the house.

Trouble in Paradise

You can't tell from here that the crawl space in this home is costing its owners extra money in heating and cooling costs and is rotting the house from the inside out.

GROUNDWATER LEAKAGE lies in a crawl space, slowly evaporating into the house.

EXPOSED EARTH adds a continuous stream of water vapor into your home.

WOOD
+ WATER
___
BAD

Block walls are porous and have lots of imperfect mortar joints in them. They suck up water from the ground, making a wet surface on the inside of the crawl space walls to evaporate into the house. Damp air from the ground passes right through the block walls. Builders do not plan for these things, and that's why they happen.

Crawl spaces often have poor or nonexistent exterior footing drains and no damp-proof or waterproof exterior wall coatings. In Oregon and other places, builders install a drain inside of crawl spaces in a low spot — obviously planning on the crawl spaces leaking, and making a way for the water to flow out. This does not help the water vapor issue one bit.

In fact, water does very little to ruin a home with a dirt crawl space. The water seldom (if ever) touches any of the parts that get ruined, such as floor joists and sill plates. It's the water vapor, also called relative humidity, that kills the house — and very few people seem to understand where this high relative humidity comes from or how to control it.

BLOCK WALLS allow water and water vapor in easily.

It's 2017. We sent a man to the moon... almost fifty years ago, but we can't figure out how to keep our houses with dirt crawl spaces from being eaten by mold and fungus. That is what this book is about. It is the biggest loophole in the building code. Plumbers, electricians, home inspectors, pest control operators, etc., crawl in these godforsaken, nasty, dirty, drafty, wet, moldy, rotting places every day. It's time we said, "This isn't right! This is bad!" We have to do something!

Water from the Air

Air is a very efficient way to move water. Air, including humid air, moves easily in and out of spaces. It's all around us and moves in vast quantities through the largest and smallest of spaces. Air brings its moisture content with it wherever it goes.

Here's the "magic," or "black magic," part. When air is heated or cooled, its relative humidity changes. Warm air holds more moisture than cold air. The relative humidity of air goes down by 2.2% for every degree (Fahrenheit) we heat it and up by 2.2% for every degree we cool it.

How Summer Venting Makes a Crawl Space Moisture Problem Worse

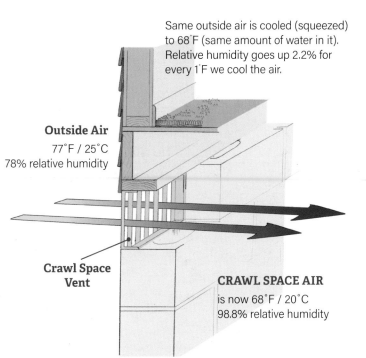

Same outside air is cooled (squeezed) to 68˚F (same amount of water in it). Relative humidity goes up 2.2% for every 1˚F we cool the air.

Outside Air
77˚F / 25˚C
78% relative humidity

Crawl Space Vent

CRAWL SPACE AIR
is now 68˚F / 20˚C
98.8% relative humidity

Ground Temperature

The average temperature of the ground in your area is the same as the average annual outdoor temperature in your area. Whatever that number is, clearly it is less than the temperature of the air that enters your crawl space in the summer.

Condensation makes everything wet | Mold is growing | Wood is rotting

Water does very little to ruin a home with a dirt crawl space. It's the water **vapor** that kills the house.

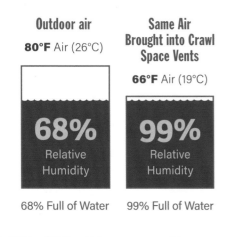

Outdoor air	Same Air Brought into Crawl Space Vents
80°F Air (26°C)	**66°F** Air (19°C)
68% Relative Humidity	**99%** Relative Humidity
68% Full of Water	99% Full of Water

Got it?

Crawl spaces are cool, because the earth is around 55°F year round (ground surface temperatures vary based on season and geography). When we bring warm, humid air into a crawl space, the air is cooled and the relative humidity goes up. High relative humidity causes rot, mold and energy loss, and attracts pests.

Here's the problem. Many years ago when some guys were writing the building code, they rationalized that since we have a lot of moisture from the ground in our dirt crawl spaces, we need to do something about it. They figured that if they vented a crawl space, the moisture would flow out through the vents.

Maybe it was too obvious. Maybe they didn't notice how it rains twice a week or so, or they didn't stop to think about what causes it to rain. Maybe it didn't occur to the authors of the building code that when it was a damp day, they would be venting the crawl space with damp air. And when it was a cold day, they would be venting the crawl space with cold air. And when it was a hot day, they'd be venting the crawl space with hot, humid air. And they certainly didn't know about, or take into account, the fact that air flows upward in a house.

On **cold days**, we are venting our crawl spaces with **cold air.**

On **hot days**, we are venting our crawl spaces with **hot air**.

On **wet days**, we are venting our crawl spaces with **wet air**.

Cinder Block Walls

Cinder block is concrete block made with the uncombusted remains of coal fires. The dark gray cinders were readily available and lightweight, but also made the blocks very porous and leaky. Cinder blocks have not been manufactured for fifty years or so.

Crawl Space Foundation Types

1. CONCRETE BLOCK WALLS

- Most common and still used today.

- Hollow and very porous.

- Block walls are the easiest and cheapest material to build a foundation with. They are also the least resistant to water and air going through them since there are so many joints in the wall. To make matters worse, each block has hollow cavities, and when the blocks are stacked on top of each other, they form a big honeycomb of air spaces. Block walls have been referred to as "God's gift to waterproofing contractors."

2. POURED CONCRETE WALLS

3. STONE WALLS

- Solid concrete.

- More common in newer homes.

- Unless there is a hole, crack or pipe penetration, water and air do not penetrate them.

- Common in older homes.

- They leak water and air.

CHAPTER TWO

THE FRESH AIR FALLACY
Venting Crawl Spaces

Most of us believe that outdoor air is healthier than indoor air. We say: "It's stuffy in here. Go out and get some fresh air."

It would seem sensible, then, to air out your crawl space. It's so damp down there — letting in some air should solve that problem. And since you're never actually down there, you might as well air it out all the time. Problem solved? Not exactly . . .

Sometimes the solution is worse than the problem.
And sometimes the solution is not a solution, and worse than the problem.
That's what venting a crawl space is.

Venting on a Hot Summer Day

When we say "relative humidity," we mean how full of water the air is relative to the maximum amount of water it can hold at a given temperature.

Let's look at what happens on a hot summer day. You have 84°F air with 75% relative humidity entering your vents. The air in your crawl space is 66°F but the surface temperature of your walls, dirt floor and floor joists is 62°F. What will happen when this air comes in (supposedly to vent the moisture out and make things better)?

Even the nontechnical person can follow this simple discussion on relative humidity and dew points. This is critical to an understanding of the vented crawl space problem.

For every one degree we cool the air, the relative humidity goes up by 2.2% because cool air holds less water than warm air. Looking at our summertime situation, there is a difference of 22°F between the outside air we are letting in at 84°F and the crawl space surfaces at 62°F. If we multiply 22°F by 2.2%, we get a 48.4% increase in relative humidity at the points where it contacts the surfaces.

Our 84°F air started out with 75% relative humidity; in other words at 84°F it was 75% full of water. Now we have cooled it to 62°F, so we have to add 48.4% to the relative humidity. That would make the relative humidity 123.4%. But wait a minute; we can't have over 100% relative humidity. Why not? Because at 100% the air cannot hold any more water and must give up its moisture.

CRAWL SPACE VENTS are a major problem.

A HYGROMETER measures relative humidity. You can buy one for as little as $19.

Vents are good for more than letting in hot, wet or cold air – they can let in water, too.

What do we mean by "give up its moisture?" We mean that it will either rain or it will come out on surfaces as condensation. When the relative humidity reaches 100%, we call this the dew point — the point at which the air gives up its moisture.

When this warm, humid air enters a crawl space, if the crawl space air were colder than the crawl space surfaces, it would rain in the crawl space. But that is never the case. The source of the cold is the earth and the source of the warmth is the air coming in from the vents, so the surfaces in your crawl space are always colder than the air in a crawl space.

So on this summer day, we get condensation, which means our crawl space walls get wet. The dirt surface of the floor gets wet. Our air ducts get wet, especially if we have the air conditioning on, which makes the ducts cold. Our cold water pipes get wet. These surfaces are the coldest.

THE CEILING, the insulation and even the light bulb drip with water as warm, humid air gives up its moisture on cool surfaces.

Our floor joists, girders, sill plates and insulation get wet with condensation. As the insulation gets wet, it gets heavy and falls to the crawl space floor.

Having high humidity in a crawl space also causes all porous material to soak up moisture from the air like a sponge. There is a direct correlation between relative humidity and wood moisture content. Wood in a damp environment will become damp itself. Damp wood rots, and mold grows on it.

The moisture content of wood is roughly proportional to the relative humidity of the surrounding air.

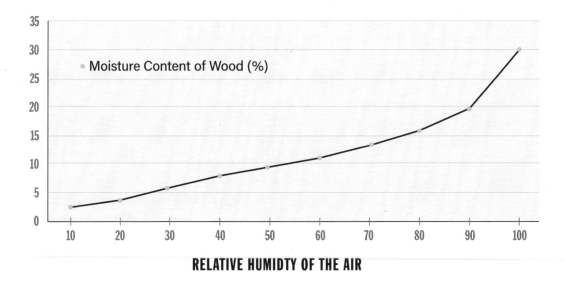

- Moisture Content of Wood (%)

RELATIVE HUMIDTY OF THE AIR

This chart shows something that is easy to understand: **the wetter the air gets, the wetter the wood gets.**

All these wet surfaces in a crawl space will eventually have to dry, and the moisture will have to go somewhere. So, let's say we had a few hot summer days, which caused condensation in our crawl space. Then the next four or five days are cooler and mild. Is the problem over? No way. After the hot days, we are left with wet crawl space surfaces everywhere. They dry into the crawl space air over the next weeks and months — and meanwhile mold and wood-destroying fungi are having a party, eating your house.

Sound the Alarm

Even the concrete beams and columns in this fire station crawl space are no match for the destructive crawl space environment.

The town spent hundreds of thousands of dollars restoring the floor system above the crawl space.

Venting on a Spring or Fall Day

Of course, my examples are for a four-season climate, typical in much of the United States. However, if you are in the Southern United States, then you know that my summer example is what you have most of the year. If you are in Maine, then you know that my summer examples are applicable for two or three months out of the year, and the winter examples are for longer periods.

If we have a day that is 72°F outside, just room temperature, and it is a humid day — say, 80% relative humidity — then when we bring this air into our crawl space to "make things better," it will cause condensation. Let's do the math: If the relative humidity (RH) is 80% and we cool the air by 10°F, then we have increased its RH by 22%, for a new RH of 102%. Since this is over 100%, then we will have condensation in our crawl space. Is this an extremely hot day? No, it's a normal room-temperature day outside and we still have a wet crawl space.

Let's say it's not so humid. Let's say that the RH outside is only 60%. When we bring our 72°F air into the crawl space, we cool it to 62°F. That's a drop of 10 °F, which will increase the RH by 22% to 82%. That's less than 100% — so we are good, right? Wrong! Mold and fungus and rot happen at over 70% RH, and some can thrive at less than that. A relative humidity of 82% in our crawl space is way more than we want, and very unhealthy.

So far, we have learned that venting doesn't work because it doesn't get rid of the dampness (and wetness) in our crawl space, but increases it instead.

SO DESPERATE were these homeowners to find a solution, they turned an entire hatchway door into a vent by putting a big screen on it. This only made the problem worse in the summer, and in the winter it froze their water pipes and caused serious heat loss.

Venting on a Cool or Winter Day

If the RH of air goes up when we cool it, it goes down when we heat it. If we vent our crawl spaces in the winter and bring in 35°F air with 60% RH, and we warm that air in our 62°F crawl space, the RH goes to 3%. With this dry air we can begin to dry our crawl space. In reality, of course, the dry, cold air mixes with the crawl space air and cools the crawl space, and we have water evaporating from the earth into the crawl space air, so we never actually achieve 3% RH in our crawl space — but materials do dry out, and there is no condensation.

Hey, we're drying our crawl space with vents now! This is great, right? Well, if you like high energy bills, cold floors and cold drafts, then this is for you! *(Read on for more information on energy penalties.)*

WHEN IT'S COLD OUT, vents let in cold air under our feet. It makes no sense!

CHAPTER THREE

WHY ARE CRAWL SPACE FLOORS DIRT ANYWAY?

And Why You Should Care

Once upon a time, all people lived in dwellings with dirt floors. Millions still do, but I don't know very many who would live that way if they had the choice. It's uncomfortable and unhealthy.

Of course, living in a house with a dirt crawl space is not the same as living on a dirt floor. True, your kitchen floor is freezing, and sometimes you pick up a musty smell from down there. But what's all the fuss about? Isn't this a perfectly acceptable way to build a house?

I have often pondered this question. All areas of the country have a mix of crawl spaces, basements and slab-on-grade construction. I come from an area where basements are more common than crawl spaces. I have often wondered: "Why do building codes treat crawl spaces differently than basements?" Aside from the variation in ceiling heights, they are not essentially different, and yet to this day, we have different codes for basements and crawl spaces.

The only reason to build a home with a dirt crawl space is to save money. A dirt crawl space floor is cheaper than a concrete floor. I guess that's the rationale behind lots of building defects. If money were not an obstacle, builders could build the perfect house. But money is an obstacle, so it's pay now or pay later for homeowners. Still, to me, the damage from dirt crawl spaces is so significant, and so expensive, that they should not be allowed.

We should never build a home with a dirt crawl space again, even if it costs a few bucks more to do it right. Simply put, a house with a dirt crawl space is dysfunctional, and a dysfunctional house is not worth building at any price.

If we think about what you would do and not do in building a basement, the same rules should apply to a crawl space. In this modern day, we would never create a dirt floor in a basement — so why do we have dirt floors in crawl spaces? We would never vent a basement, so why vent a crawl space?

If you went down into a friend's basement in the winter and saw a window open, or many windows open for that matter, you'd tell your friend, "Close the windows, it's cold down here!" You might even add the word dummy. Yet we put big holes in our crawl space walls and accept it as normal in the name of "making things better." It does not make things better. The emperor has no clothes!

A HOUSE WITH A DIRT CRAWL SPACE IS DYSFUNCTIONAL,
and a dysfunctional house is not worth building at any price.

Like a Cave?

Some have said their crawl spaces are like caves. But since there is not rotting organic material in caves, the air quality in a cave is much better than most crawl spaces.

But I Never Go Down There, So Why Should I Care?

Many homeowners (I'd bet most) know their crawl space is nasty, so they never go down there. I don't blame them. In fact, I've never seen a dirt crawl space (that hasn't been retrofitted) where I crawled in and said "Heyyyy, this is pretty nice." I never even said, "Heyyyy, this is okay." It's always bad. Often really bad.

MOLD GROWING on a door upstairs from a wet summer crawl space.

Homeowners know this and don't go down into their crawl space unless they absolutely have to. They shut it out of their "often visited places in my house" list, and shut it out of their mind, like it doesn't exist. Hey, if I don't go down there, what do I care? Right? Wrong. Way wrong.

If you care about how much you pay for heating and cooling, then you care about your crawl space. If you care about your home rotting, or mold, allergies or asthma, then you care about your crawl space. If you care about the comfort of your home, cold floors, drafts and how your home smells, then you care about your crawl space. If you care how long the paint lasts on your house, about doors and windows sticking, about hardwood floors buckling and carpets going moldy, then you care about your crawl space. If you care about your resale value, then you care about your crawl space. You can't get away from it. The house is one building. It operates as a system. You can't have one part of the building that is sick and another part that is healthy. You can't rationalize that since you never go in the crawl space you aren't affected by it. Why? Simple. Air mixing.

The crawl space air is bad. It is damp. It is cold if it's winter. It is full of mold spores. It smells. And this crawl space air is in your building envelope. It gets upstairs in one of two ways: the stack effect (explained on next page), or via the HVAC system courtesy of your ducts. You are breathing it. In fact, we know that one-third to one-half of the air that you breathe on the first floor of your house came through your crawl space. (By the way, this goes for basements, too.)

This fact has been proven by studies. If someone sprays paint inside your crawl space, do you think you'd smell the spray paint upstairs? Of course you would.

Radon gas is a naturally occurring radioactive gas that comes from the ground. For many years, we have known that if you measure the radon levels in your basement or crawl space, and then measure upstairs, you will have about one-third the amount upstairs. Since radon only comes from the ground, this demonstrates how air moves in a house from bottom to top.

Moisture inside your home is bad for what's in it.

You Breathe Crawl Space Air — Like It or Not

As warm air rises in a home, it leaks out of the upper levels. New air must enter to replace the air that escaped. In fact, in a tight home about half of the air escapes each hour out of the upper levels. This creates a suction at the lower levels to draw in replacement air. In older, leaky homes, the air exchange rate can be as high as two full air exchanges per hour.

This *stack effect* creates an airflow in your home from bottom to top. Air from the basement is drawn upward into the first floor, and then to the second floor. Of course, it dilutes with other air in your home, but building scientists say that up to 50% of the air you breathe on the first floor is air that came from the crawl space. If you have hot air heating with ductwork, the air mixes even more thoroughly throughout the house.

Therefore, whatever is in your crawl space air is in your house and affecting you, whether or not you spend any time in the crawl space. If there is high humidity downstairs, there is higher humidity upstairs than there would be otherwise. If there is mold in the crawl space, there are mold spores upstairs. If there are damp odors in your crawl space . . . you get the idea.

Air leaking out causes air to leak in.

STACK EFFECT

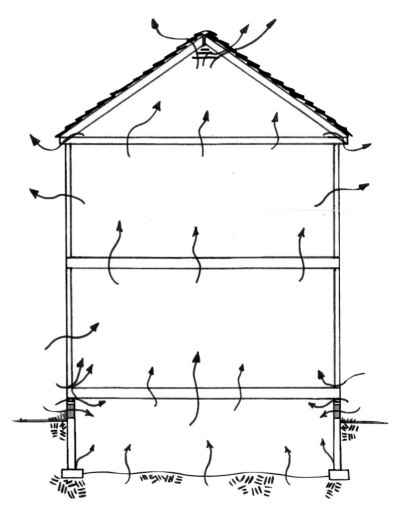

The idea behind vented crawl spaces — that we can expect air to flow in through vents on one side of the house and out through vents on the other side — is a bunch of baloney. What actually happens is that air enters the vents in the front, enters the vents in the back and enters the vents on the sides, and then it goes up!

HOW LONG DO YOU WANT YOUR HOME TO LAST?

The vented dirt crawl space has sentenced this new home to an early demise.

Some say that on a windy day the air flows through a crawl space via the vents. The problem is you would need wind every day for this to be effective. And then there's the downside: wind depressurizes the whole building, sucking air out of it at a faster rate than it blows it in. This creates a need for more replacement air to make up for the air that left. So we suck more air up from the vented crawl space on a windy day.

Besides, even if vents made air flow through a crawl space on a windy day, you would just be making warm, humid air or very cold air flow through your house faster because of the wind. Venting a crawl space doesn't make sense unless the outdoor air is 70˚F and 45% RH day and night, all year long. So it doesn't make sense.

How does the air get from the crawl space up into the house (besides ducts)? Air is a very small thing. With this driving mechanism (the suction of the house at the ground level), air is drawn up through every tiny opening between the crawl space and your house: holes around wires and pipes, joints in floor boards, space around access hatches and through duct chases. You can seal these openings, but you can never get it perfect, so you can't stop it.

Venting

Venting doesn't make sense unless the outdoor air is 70°F with a relative humidity of 45%, day and night, year-round.

Increased
Energy Bills

Damp air takes more energy to cool in the summer and heat in the winter.

"Just Add Water"
Negative Effects of a Wet or Damp Crawl Space

Since air flows into the upper levels of your home from the crawl space, it brings the humidity from the crawl space with it. The effects on your home can include:

- **Dust mites** (the number one indoor allergen)
- **Sticking** (swollen) doors and windows
- **Smelly damp carpets**
- **Buckling hardwood floors**
- **Condensation/rotting/mold in your attic** (as humid air escapes into your attic it can condense against the cold ceiling or roof)
- **Frost or condensation and mold** on the inside of windows in cool weather
- **Increased cooling bills** (damp air takes more energy to cool)
- **Increased heating bills** (damp air takes more energy to heat)
- **Mold upstairs**
- **Decreased life of roof sheathing and shingles**
- **Decreased life of the paint on the outside of your house**
- **Aggravated asthma and allergies**

The damage in the crawl space itself is obvious. The above list represents many effects that can happen upstairs, which you may not associate with your wet or damp crawl space.

Ducts bring crawl space air upstairs easily.

▼

If you have ducts in your crawl space (which most do) then you have a built-in air highway to efficiently mix all the air in your home, from crawl space to the upper floor. How? It's simple: **duct leakage.**

Air Mixing Through Your Ducts

(Skip this section if you have hot water heat)

Ducts are made of segments of sheet metal, or combinations of sheet metal, duct board and flex duct. Between the sections and at the elbows there are joints which are simply bent, crimped or screwed together.

Supply ducts are under pressure, blowing the air that you pay to heat and cool from your heating and cooling equipment to the rooms you want to heat and cool. As this pressurized air passes by loose joints and seams in the duct, a little air leaks out. Okay, so it's only 2% of the air in the duct. No biggie, right? Well, what about the next joint? Oops, 2% of the remaining air leaks out. And the next and the next... it adds up. When you have a lot of supply duct leakage, a couple of things happen. You depressurize the living spaces above and pressurize the crawl space. This pushes the damp, smelly, moldy air from the crawl space up into the living spaces faster than it would move in that direction otherwise. It's a no-win situation. It costs you money and you and your family breathe diluted crawl space air all day.

Return ducts suck air from the rooms you want to heat and cool, and send it back to the heating/cooling unit. They run through the crawl space, and when they leak, they suck the bad air from the crawl space directly into your duct system, and blow it right back into the house. So that's a losing situation, too.

The average home with ducts has 300 cubic feet per minute of duct leakage. One possible solution is to seal the ducts. Before you do, you should finish reading this book, because your crawl space and the bad effects it has on your house can be fixed without doing this.

Sealed duct systems do exist, but you have a better chance of seeing Bigfoot. A contractor would use duct mastic (not duct tape, which is good for everything except sealing ducts) and paint the stuff on every joint in the duct system. An arduous process, indeed — especially when you're lying on your back in the mud, with spider webs in your hair.

◀ **IF THAT'S ON THE OUTSIDE OF THE DUCT, WHAT'S ON THE INSIDE?**

Ducts in a Crawl Space

More Bad News

When warm, humid air enters crawl space vents, where is the first place it will give up its moisture? On the coldest surfaces, right? The coldest surface is likely to be your ducts when the air conditioning is on. Water is a conductor, not an insulator. So when a duct is wet, it is warmed by the summer air that came through the crawl space vents.

A friend of mine, Royce Lewis at Comfort Diagnostics in Little Rock, Arkansas, measured the air coming out of an air conditioning unit at 55°F. Then he measured the temperature at the other end of the duct line, where the air was vented into the room, and the air was 65°F! The AC unit was cooling the air by 20°F — from 75°F to 55°F — but the air was back up to 65°F by the time it got back into the room. That's a full 50% energy loss! Why? The duct was wet and running through a warmer space.

Here's more bad news for those of you who heat your homes. You wouldn't purify water and send it through dirty pipes before you drink it, right? Yet we heat our air and send it through cold ducts to our rooms. The ducts are thin sheet metal, sometimes with thin insulation, most of the times with no insulation. We have open vents in our crawl space and it's 30°F out. So the ducts are cold. You lose again. I know it's disheartening and frustrating, but there is a solution. *Read on...*

◀ **DUCTS THAT ARE WET FROM CONDENSATION ROB YOU OF ENERGY.**

Higher Energy Bills

From Your Dirt Crawl Space

A home with a dirt crawl space costs more to heat and cool. Besides all the reasons we already mentioned, there are other factors working against you. If your crawl space is vented, those vents make your floors cold upstairs. This is not only uncomfortable, but it means that it will cost more to heat your house.

Houses with dirt crawl spaces have damp air. Damp air uses more energy to heat and cool, and more energy costs more money. Damp air puts more of a latent (hidden) load on the HVAC system. Everyone knows they need to run their AC more on a humid day. But what about humidity from inside the building? Same thing. If you get rid of the humidity from your crawl space, you save money on heating and cooling costs.

How much money? You will save 15% to 25%*. That's a lot of money! Over the years, it really adds up. Every month you are paying the price for living in a house with a dirt crawl space. Of course, there are variables, such as how many vents you have, whether you live in a one- or two-story home, whether you have ducts in the crawl space, how big your crawl space is, et cetera.

These penalties for living with the dirt crawl space problem, and the savings from fixing it, are real and proven.

DIRT CRAWL SPACES make the air in your house damp – and damp air costs more to heat and cool

$ Fixing your crawl space is one home repair you can't afford not to make.

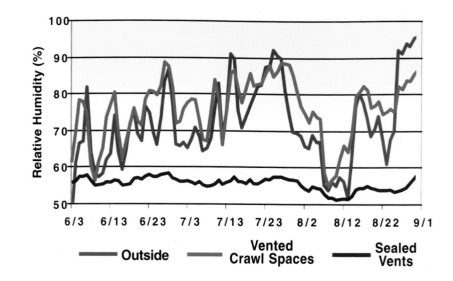

Crawl Space RH (Summer 2002)

Comparing the relative humidity levels in sealed unvented crawl spaces, vented dirt crawl spaces, and outdoors.

This chart clearly shows that sealed, unvented crawl spaces have far less moisture in them, ending any lingering debate on the venting issue.

In fact, the energy loss is so substantial in a home with a vented dirt crawl space and ducts that you may as well ignore all other ways to save energy and make your home more comfortable until you fix the crawl space problem. Caulking around a window or weather-stripping a door would be like patching a tiny hole in a rowboat and ignoring the foot-wide hole on the other side.

Controlling air infiltration is the key to energy conservation in a building. Your top priority is to close up those giant holes in your crawl space walls while also eliminating the reason (exposed damp earth) that those holes were put there in the first place.

If light can get in, so can air.

With the lights off, you can see sunlight around this crawl space access door. Air leaks like this, where outside air can enter a crawl space, must be sealed to get control of the indoor environment.

It doesn't take long before the numbers add up to serious money. If you combine that with the benefits of preserving your home's value by eliminating the need for rot repairs and mold remediation, you can see that fixing your crawl space is one home repair you can't afford not to make.

Spread across the 26 million homes with dirt crawl spaces, it is estimated that with just a 15% energy savings, homeowners in the U.S. alone would save $7 billion annually. That's a lot of money that could be better spent somewhere else!

Vent Covers

The CleanSpace vent cover seals crawl space vents permanently from the outside to stop unwanted outside air from entering the crawl space, while covering ugly vents with an attractive panel. The available colors of black and gray match a home's foundation nicely.

Sealing Vents

Basement Systems, Inc., has developed permanent gasketed vent covers to stop unwanted outside air.

An Insulation Diaper

The plastic facing on this insulation prevents it from drying. It gets heavy and droops down, making an air space between it and the floor above. It has almost no thermal benefit at all. This is common with paper- and foil-faced insulation as well.

Insulation Myths

Some crawl spaces have insulation in the floor above (that is, in the ceiling of the crawl space), and some do not. A few important points need to be made.

First, one reason for insulation in the floor above is that the crawl space is cold in the winter due to the open vents. If these vents were closed permanently, it would make a huge difference in the temperature of the floor above.

Second, fiberglass insulation only works in a closed cavity. Fiberglass insulation is loose and air passes right through it. When it's positioned between the joists in a vented crawl space, with the paper or foil side up and the unfaced side down, it's not doing much at all.

Oh, yes, about that facing: Paper-faced insulation is mold candy — a term I borrow from Joe Lstiburek from Building Science Corp. Mold loves paper even more than wood.

Foil-faced insulation is supposed to be a radiant barrier. You face the foil toward the heated side — but you need at least ½ inch of air space in front of foil radiant barriers for them to reflect the heat. Whenever I see foil-faced insulation used in a crawl space ceiling, the radiant barrier is jammed up against the floor sheathing with no air space between the facing and the sheathing. Therefore, that element of the insulation is not working. Besides, such an air space, if it were provided in the open cavity between floor joists, would create a thermal bypass where air can flow on both sides of the insulation, rendering it useless. Mold grows on fiberglass insulation because it has some organic material in the resin used to set the fibers.

A last important note: When fiberglass insulation is just a little damp, it loses a whole lot of its insulation value.

So what is your fiberglass insulation doing in your dirt crawl space? Not much.

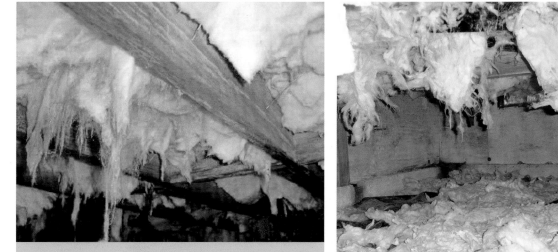

FIBERGLASS INSULATION does little when it's either not in a closed cavity or when it's damp.

MOLD LOVES paper facing on insulation

Fiberglass floor insulation and moisture: **a very bad combination**

Insulation should always be installed against the air boundary surface of the house. In a healthy, properly functioning crawl space, that surface is the crawl space walls and floors. The wood floor system above is full of gaps, joints and chases for wires, pipes and ducts, so it's not the air boundary, and it's the wrong place to insulate in a crawl space with no vents. By sealing all outside air leaks and insulating the walls (and even the floor), you can make the crawl space part of the conditioned space of the house and a very friendly place for ducts. Read on...

CHAPTER FOUR

CRAWL SPACE BIOLOGY
Mold, Fungus, Rot – and Critters

Beyond the cold and the moisture and the dirt, it's the living organisms in your crawl space —
the fungus and the insects — that could end up literally eating you out of house and home.

Wet load-bearing girders and floor joists are under attack by mold.
Soon this framing will get so rotted it will all need to be replaced.

Mold has become a big issue in recent years. Mold is the subject of lawsuits, a terror to builders, subject matter for front-page writers, the reason for school closings and the growth of an industry: mold testing and remediation. With all this talk about mold, you might think it is new. It is not new. You might think it is a complex issue. It is not a complex issue; it is actually very simple.

First, let's talk about why mold exists. Mold has a purpose. Its purpose is to break down or eat dead organic matter. That's what it's here for. Without mold, plant and animal material would grow and grow and pile up and pile up.

Mold Intelligence

Mold knows why it was put here. If a material is organic, dead and wet, mold knows to eat it. Organic material in a building is anything that was once living, such as wood. Mold sends out its spores everywhere, and they can lie dormant for many years. When the spores encounter something that is organic, dead and wet, mold grows on it and eats it. When we say "mold," we mean any mold or other fungus, of which there are many thousands of varieties.

Since mold spores are everywhere, and our building materials and the contents of our homes (furniture, boxes, clothes, etc.) are made from organic materials, this factor cannot be controlled. The only factor that we can control in our homes is the moisture.

Most molds need 70% relative humidity (RH) to grow. It's important to remember that it's the moisture level on the surface of the organic material, not the level in the air, that triggers mold growth. In a crawl space, the RH of the surfaces is often higher than the RH of the surrounding air because the temperature of the surfaces is lower than the temperature of the air.

Mold likes processed organic fibers best. It will grow on paper and cardboard first (remember, paper is like "mold candy"). After that it will grow on fiberboard and chipboard, and then plywood, and finally on framing lumber. Drywall has paper on it. Mold loves drywall.

Mold releases airborne spores, which are so light they float on the slightest air currents, off to find more suitable places to grow. Most people are not allergic to mold spores, but some are. The higher the concentration of mold spores, the greater percentage of people who will be bothered by them.

There is plenty of information out there on the health effects of mold — but they will not be explained here. One thing is for sure: mold growing in your house is not good. It's not good for your health, and it is increasingly not good for your property value. Who wants to buy a house with mold? Nobody.

NO LAUGHING MATTER
It's just a matter of time before a damp crawl space rots your floor out.

DAMP LEATHER
Sound the mold dinner bell!

THE SILL PLATE ROTTING right over this vent is no coincidence. It's ironic that the problem wasn't fixed after the sill was replaced.

To Your Health
(and if not yours, then theirs)

You can't find a doctor who says mold in a home is good. You can't find a doctor who says mold in your home is not bad. It's bad. It's all bad.

Besides irritating people with asthma and mold allergies, studies show that prolonged exposure to mold can actually cause asthma.

Mold = Bad

MOLD

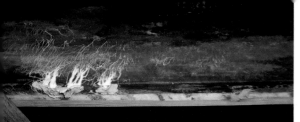

Meet Your Sister

The practice of nailing a new floor joist alongside a structurally compromised old one is called sistering. This is done because the subfloor above, as well as wiring and plumbing, are secured to the old joist, so it's nearly impossible to remove.

Sistering may restore structural strength to the joist, but it leaves the old rotting joist in place. Soon the sister will get moldy, too. And what about the rotted plywood subfloor above? Unless the real problem — the moisture — is fixed, it seems inevitable that many of these homes will be condemned in the future. What do you think?

The waterproofing industry is not the only one that has vented dirt crawl spaces to thank for a significant part of its annual revenue. Contractors who make structural repairs to replace floor joists, girders, and sill plates — basically the entire floor framing system under your house — are kept very busy repairing the damage caused by mold and rot.

These repairs aren't cheap. In fact, they can be very expensive. You can imagine a carpenter figuring out how he's going to crawl under your home and get new 16-foot-long 2 x 10s in place, with all the duct work, wiring, plumbing, and bridging (cross bracing) that are attached to the old rotted joists, all while operating on his back in a low crawl space. It's not easy on him, and it's not going to be easy on your bank account.

To compound the expense, most of the time, these structural repairs are done without ever fixing the underlying moisture problem! So it's only a matter of time before the new framing rots out and has to be done again.

What is the designed lifespan of a house? In other words, how long do you want your house to last without needing major repairs? If the answer is longer than 10, 15 or 25 years, then you had better fix your dirt crawl space.

When you look at the cost of higher energy bills — and then add in the cost of rot repairs that eventually will have to be done — you can easily see that it is more expensive to live with a dirt crawl space than to fix it. By not fixing your dirt crawl space, over the life of the house, you will pay many times more than it costs to fix now.

WHEN THE FLOORS IN NEARLY ALL 36 UNITS in this New England condominium complex began bouncing and getting soft, they realized the crawl spaces were a bigger problem than they thought. As an emergency measure, they had to sister new framing lumber to each side of every girder and every floor joist so the homes would not cave in. Eventually they hired Basement Systems to install a CleanSpace Crawl Space Encapsulation System to fix the moisture problem.

No Joke

These joists appear to melt into a softening sill plate as they rot. Not to mention, termites love wet wood. You can see the remnants of a termite tunnel up the wall here in this photo.

When BX cable rusts out, the electrical ground is lost — a very dangerous situation.

WHAT'S CHEAPER: replacing the floors and paying higher energy bills, or fixing the dirt crawl space? **ANSWER:** fixing your dirt crawl space.

Dust Mites and Other Critters Love Your Dirt Crawl Space

The number one allergen that people with asthma and allergies react to is dust mite droppings. Dust mites are microscopic parasites that live off of skin flakes that you shed. They live in your bedding, your carpet and your furniture. Dust mite droppings are tiny and float in the air, where they can be breathed in and aggravate allergies and asthma. For more excellent and easy-to-understand information, visit housedustmite.com.

Dust mites do not drink water but absorb it from the air. They need over 50% relative humidity to live. While dust mites do not live in your crawl space, they like your crawl space. Why? It is very difficult to keep your house dry when you have a dirt crawl space under it. It's this life-giving humidity that allows dust mites to thrive upstairs. Dry the crawl space out and the air flowing up into the house is no longer wet. Therefore, the house dries out. The dust mites (which are like tiny water balloons) dry out and die and, of course, stop pooping. That's great news for allergy and asthma sufferers.

Other pests love the moisture in the crawl space, too. Termites love wet wood. Spiders love crawl spaces, because spiders eat other bugs and there are usually plenty of them in a nice damp dirt crawl space.

Mice and rats like dirt crawl spaces, and so do snakes and all kinds of other creatures. And when the time comes, a dirt crawl space is often a nice peaceful place to go to die — and subsequently decompose. Blessed are crawl space workers who can go in and do their job without being creeped out!

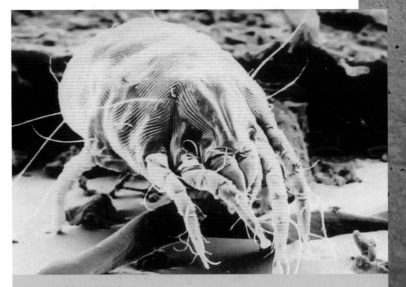

DUST MITES live upstairs and thrive in humid environments. Their droppings are the number one indoor allergen.

MICE are very happy to live and die in your dirt crawl space

47

What's That White Chalky Powder?

When the minerals in concrete, mortar or soil dissolve in water, they can end up as deposits on the surface of a wall or floor. When the water evaporates, it leaves the minerals behind. This mineral residue manifests as white powder or crystals known as efflorescence. It is sometimes confused with mold, but it is not alive. Efflorescence is not harmful (unless you eat it) and can be easily swept or brushed off. It is a sign that water is (probably slowly) coming through the concrete.

That White Chalky Powder on Your Walls is Efflorescence

BEFORE

AFTER

Solutions

Fixing your dirt crawl space problem delivers a lot of benefits, without requiring you to undertake a terribly expensive and disruptive home improvement project.

There are four steps to totally eliminate any negative effects on the rest of the house caused by your dirt crawl space.

Step 1:
Fix the water leakage (if there is any)

Step 2:
Isolate the house from the earth

Step 3:
Seal the vents and other outside air leaks.

Step 4:
"Condition" or dehumidify your crawl space air

CHAPTER FIVE

THE SOLUTION, STEP 1
Fix the Groundwater Leakage

• •

I have nothing against water, mind you. After all, 71% of Earth's surface is covered by the stuff. If you dig a deep enough hole anywhere on the planet, water will try to fill it, and if we're talking about a bathtub or a swimming pool, I'm all for it.

In fact, you need water to live, but not in your crawl space. **Here's how to get it out — and keep it out.**

Some crawl spaces don't leak when it rains hard. If this is you, go to Step 2. If your crawl space does leak when it rains hard, even if it's only once in a while, then you have to do something to control the groundwater before you can hope to fix your overall crawl space problem.

If you don't know whether your crawl space leaks, do a careful inspection to look for signs of water pooling in the low areas. Most crawl spaces have a low spot, or perhaps several areas that are lower than the rest. Look in these areas carefully with a good light. If water ponds there (even if it's only once every few years), you will see signs of that happening. Look for waterlines (rings of silt and fine soil particles that washed down to the low areas) or erosion patterns in the soil where the water made its way from its entry point to the low spot. I have seen crawl spaces that leak very badly, getting up to a foot of water in spaces that are only 24 inches high to begin with! Others leak much less dramatically.

The first thing that must be done is the installation of a sump pump. To install one, a hole must be dug that is 22 inches deep and at least as wide at the low spot of the crawl space. In the rest of the crawl space, the soil should be moved as needed to fill other low areas, or to crown the middle a bit. The idea is to have the crawl space floor pitch down, even if only slightly, toward the sump hole, and not have other low areas where water can puddle.

The next thing to do is install a sump liner in the hole to keep the mud out, providing a nice clean housing for the pump.

A specially designed crawl space sump system has features such as:

1. **A sturdy liner** made to mate with an airtight lid

2. **A floor drain in the lid** in case of a plumbing leak

3. **A reliable cast-iron pump** with mechanical float switch

4. **A stand** under the pump

5. **An alarm** to alert you to pump failure or a plumbing leak

STANDING WATER needs to be addressed before you can fix your overall crawl space problem.

OPEN SUMP HOLES are useless in stopping water vapor from rising from the ground.

A Smart Sump

A high-quality sump system is essential and must include a perforated sump liner, reliable pump, alarm system, pump stand, check valve, and airtight lid with a floor drain. Basement Systems' SmartSump system is shown here.

Some crawl spaces exist because there is a rock ledge that the builder did not have the means or desire to remove to dig a basement. In some cases with rock ledge, you cannot get a sump hole 22 inches deep and have to settle for digging as deep as you can — 10 inches being an absolute minimum.

The sump liner should be sturdy and have lots of holes in it to allow water from the ground to enter and be pumped out. It should also accept an airtight lid. Because you are trying to completely dry the crawl space out, a sturdy and airtight sump lid is very important. You don't want an open hole with water sitting in it, to evaporate up into your crawl space environment.

The pump is next. I recommend a 1/3 hp cast iron pump with a mechanical float switch. Pumps with pressure switches or **"ball on a wire"** switches should be avoided. A **check valve** (one-way valve) should be installed on the discharge line very close to the pump. The discharge pipe should be 1 ½-inch PVC pipe that runs to the exterior of the house.

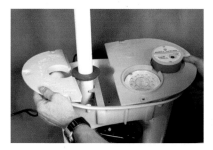

A proper discharge line location will vary from property to property. The idea is to get the water to run to a place in the yard where it will continue its flow downhill and away from the house. If you have good pitch away from your house then you may not need to run it very far. If your yard is relatively flat, then you may have to run it farther. We have run discharge lines from 3 to 103 feet away from a foundation, with 15 feet as an average.

Some pumps don't run very often and it's not a big issue, and others run quite often. The good news is that you can always extend or move the sump discharge location later if the first location proves to be unsuitable.

A really smart sump system. Specially designed for crawl spaces, the SmartSump pumps the water out of this crawl space automatically (shown with the UltraSump battery backup sump pump system).

There are a few other important elements to a proper sump installation in your crawl space:

 **Pump Stand**

 **Pump Alarm**

 **Floor Drain**

A CleanPump stand will elevate the pump above the bottom of the sump liner a bit, allowing for some sediment, mud, debris or gravel to settle to the bottom without clogging or otherwise affecting the pump. It also keeps the check valve and discharge pipe clean. A check valve (one-way valve) should be installed on all sump pump discharge lines, so that when the pump shuts off the water in the pipe doesn't flow back into the sump hole, to be pumped again on the next cycle.

How would you know if your sump pump had failed and you were in danger of being flooded? Unless you have an alarm, the answer is: when your crawl space is already flooded — which is just what you are trying to avoid. A battery-powered alarm that sounds automatically when the water reaches a level above the point where the pump(s) should normally turn on is essential. The patented WaterWatch alarm does just that: it tells you there is a problem, giving you a chance to do something about it. The SmartSump is designed just for crawl spaces, and when there is a plumbing leak in your crawl space, its alarm will sound to tell you so. Perfect!

An alarm to tell you there is a plumbing leak is only part of the answer. Not if but when you have a plumbing leak, you don't want your plastic-lined crawl space to fill with water like a swimming pool. You want the water to go down into the sump hole instead. The problem is that the sump has an airtight lid on it. The solution: a floor drain in the airtight lid that lets water go down but doesn't let damp air rise. The SmartSump has just such a drain!

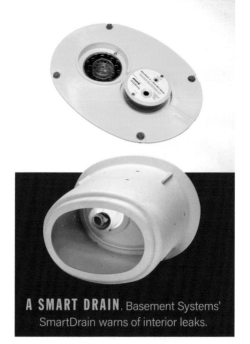

Many crawl spaces I have worked in have plumbing leaks that the homeowner never knew about because the water was soaking into the dirt floor. After we install our CleanSpace lining (which we will discuss later) in their crawl space, we see the drips on top of it and tell them about it so they can get a plumber in to fix the leak. Even if you don't need a sump pump in your crawl space, a SmartDrain alarm and drain unit should be installed.

Our Basement Systems SmartSump has all the components specifically designed to meet all the important criteria detailed here.

Once the sump liner is installed, the space between the sump liner and the hole in the ground is filled to the top with clean stone aggregate. This "stone zone" allows water from the surface of the dirt (under your crawl space liner — which is the next step) to drain down into it and through the holes in the sump liner to be pumped out.

What if my pump fails? What if the power goes out?

These are questions you should be asking yourself. After all, if you want your crawl space dry ALL the time, you're not going to get it if you don't plan on...

- The power going out one day — which usually happens in a big rainstorm
- The circuit breaker tripping
- The primary pump failing
- The primary pump not being able to keep up with the amount of water in a very heavy rain
- The pump coming unplugged

Remember all the stories of woe people have told you about getting flooded when their sump pump failed? These are the reasons behind those failures. You don't have to go through that if you get the right equipment.

Plumbing Leak Protection

Water from future plumbing leaks must be considered — it will happen one day.

ONE-WAY. An airtight sump lid with a drain keeps water vapor sealed in, while allowing water to drain down in the event of a plumbing leak.

Is a Generator an Option?

A generator is a good idea if you have an automatic one permanently installed that senses when the power goes out and starts up automatically. It needs to be wired by an electrician. A typical generator can be hooked up to run your sump pump, a few lights, the furnace and the fridge. This costs between $7,000 and $10,000 in most cases. If you go this route, be sure to install two AC primary pumps to cover you in case of pump failure, as a generator only eliminates the need for the DC backup pump.

You can purchase a portable generator for $400 or so. However, you must be home (and awake) to notice when the power fails. Then you must drag the generator outside, gas it up, start it up, and run an extension cord to your sump pump. This is not a good option.

Unless you have an automatic generator for backup power in your home, a battery-backup sump pump system, such as our UltraSump, is highly recommended. This system includes a second DC-operated pump, a second switch, a special long-term standby battery, and a matched smart charging system and control unit. If the water rises above the point where the primary pump should turn on for any reason, including a power outage, then the secondary pump will automatically operate to pump the water out. In addition, there is an alarm that alerts you that the pump is running on battery power, so if there is a malfunction with the primary pump, or there is no power to the primary pump, you have time to get it going again before the battery goes dead.

AC/DC

AC = (Alternating Current) Plugged into the wall — runs off house power

DC = (Direct Current) Runs off battery power

Basement Systems' SmartSump with an UltraSump

A battery back-up pumping system automatically pumps the water in the event of a power failure, an unplugged pump or a tripped circuit breaker.

In many crawl spaces — probably most — the pump will be all the drainage you need before going to Step 2, in which you install a crawl space liner. This depends on the grade in your crawl space. Remember that the water comes in at the perimeter of the crawl space. We don't need to keep the dirt floor dry, as we would need to keep a basement floor dry if we were waterproofing a basement. We just need to keep the water from puddling and allow it to run to the sump location. If we can regrade with a small rake or hoe to make paths for the water to flow to the sump location, then that's fine.

Another option is to dig a shallow trench at the perimeter to make the water flow to the sump location. In level crawl spaces, you can dig a deeper trench and install a SmartPipe. SmartPipe's custom design has holes on the top and front under a filter fabric, to accept water from the soil and the surface of your crawl space. There is a special flange with spacers on the back, and large holes to accept water from the crawl space walls and the joint between the footing and the wall. SmartPipe will collect the water from the perimeter of your crawl space and drain it to a sump pump location, such as the SmartSump, designed specifically for crawl spaces.

Besides the water, you must remove the water vapor.

Sump Pump Discharge Lines

Terminating the discharge line in your yard can be done in a variety of ways, but in most cases, is best accomplished with a LawnScape outlet. This durable fitting diffuses the discharge water while camouflaging the end of the pipe.

LAWNSCAPE OUTLET

NO DICE. Someone thought that a drainage trench was a good idea in this crawl space. But without a completely sealed encapsulation system to seal the dirt and separate the house from the earth, it did nothing to solve the moisture problem.

WATER VAPOR NEEDS TO BE ADDRESSED. Some crawl spaces have a layer of gravel on the dirt floor. This does nothing to stop the water vapor from rising into the house. These homes will need a sealed liner encapsulation system.

1 +1 = 1

If you have more than one AC pump to get more water out in a big rain, it makes no sense to hook them up to one discharge pipe. Using the "ten pounds of stuff in a five-pound bag" logic, you can't get more water out with two pumps unless you have two discharge pipes to the outside.

The TripleSafe twin liner, lids, CleanPump stands, bridge, etc., are all specially engineered to work together.

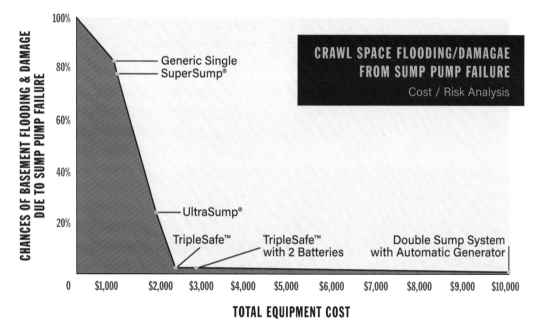

CRAWL SPACE FLOODING/DAMAGAE FROM SUMP PUMP FAILURE
Cost / Risk Analysis

Chart axes: CHANCES OF BASEMENT FLOODING & DAMAGE DUE TO SUMP PUMP FAILURE (vertical, 0–100%); TOTAL EQUIPMENT COST (horizontal, 0–$10,000). Labels: Generic Single, SuperSump®, UltraSump®, TripleSafe™, TripleSafe™ with 2 Batteries, Double Sump System with Automatic Generator.

For Those with Zero Tolerance for Crawl Space Water

To reduce your chances of getting flooded from pump failure down to a statistically insignificant number, you'll need the best sump pumping system available: the TripleSafe Sump Pump System, which sports three pumps in one sump liner.

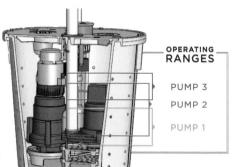

OPERATING RANGES

PUMP 3
PUMP 2
PUMP 1

Pump 1 is a high-quality, very efficient ⅓ hp Zoeller pump. It will do the lion's share of the pumping.

Pump 2 is a ½ hp Zoeller pump set a bit higher in the sump hole. It turns on in the event that the first pump fails or can't keep up with the volume of water. This second pump is more powerful and has a separate discharge line to give you that "turbo boost" in those rare cases when you need it.

Pump 3 is an UltraSump DC (battery-operated) pump that kicks in if the power goes out. It is available with one or two specially designed batteries to pump out more than 12,000 or `24,000 gallons of water respectively.

Freezing Discharge Lines

Your sump pump gets the water out of the crawl space and away from your house with a pipe — usually plastic and usually about 1½ inches in diameter. This pipe runs on the surface of the ground, or in a shallow buried trench, and discharges the water onto the surface away from the house.

The problem is that, in winter, the outlet of the pipe becomes blocked with snow and ice. When the pump runs, it fills the pipe with water (10 feet of 1½-inch pipe holds 1 gallon of water). Since the water can't get out of the pipe due to the ice at the outlet, the whole pipe fills with water and freezes. Now your pump runs, but cannot get the water out, and your crawl space floods. Just what you were trying to avoid!

Basement Systems has a solution: the IceGuard system. This is a specially engineered fitting that goes outside your home and automatically ejects the water away from the exterior wall in the event that the pipe freezes. It is designed with holes to allow this to happen, yet no water at all gets out of these openings when the pipe is not frozen.

Electrical Outlets

Electrical outlets are usually not included in your waterproofing contractor's scope of work. Although your waterproofer will leave with your sumps operational, plan on having an electrician wire a proper outlet at the sump location right after the waterproofer is done.

If you have more than one AC pump (as with a TripleSafe system), two outlets on two different circuits will ensure that you still have one AC pump operational if a circuit breaker trips.

SNOW, NO PROBLEM. The patented IceGuard solves the problem of frozen discharge lines.

With a **TRIPLESAFE PUMP SYSTEM**, both discharge lines are protected by the IceGuard system.

WATER FLOWS DOWNHILL

Dirt Around a Foundation Settles

When the loose soil is pushed back against a new foundation, it will settle — especially in the first few years. This doesn't help a wet crawl space situation, and dirt should be added so water does not flow toward the foundation. Unlike dirt, mulch is porous and water easily passes through it, so mulch doesn't count.

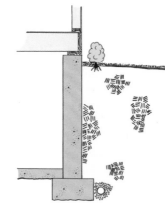

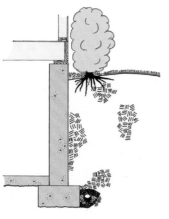

HOUSE AGE: 3 Months   **HOUSE AGE:** 7 Years

GRADING

If the soil around your foundation is pitched toward the foundation, it's a good idea to add dirt so that the soil slopes away. Be sure not to use sand or mulch, because water flows right down through these materials whether they are pitched or not. It's best to use clay or other dense dirt.

Be sure that you keep the dirt at least four inches down from the siding. If the siding is close to or touching the soil, it will rot and you'll have another problem. Termites could also create a highway into your home undetected.

Downspouts

You didn't need to read a book to have someone tell you to keep your gutters from dumping water next to your foundation, did you? I only have to state it so someone doesn't say my book is incomplete without this obvious advice.

So how do you do it? There are a few alternatives to laying ugly pipes and contraptions across your lawn that get in the way of mowing and your annual croquet game at the family picnic.

One solution is to bury pipes from the downspouts underground away from the foundation. Rather than having an ugly pipe sticking out in your yard, the pipes can terminate on the surface with a durable, dark-green water dispersion fitting called a LawnScape Outlet. The cover unscrews to enable the removal of any debris that may collect inside.

There are a few other options that work very well. A product called RainChute is recessed into the ground just an inch or so, and takes the water up to 7 feet away. Usually this is all you need to make a big difference. The advantage of RainChute is that it is not above grade to cause a tripping or mowing problem. It is not unsightly, yet it is not underground either, so it's not expensive and won't clog.

For areas that are landscaped and don't need mowing, a simple extension called RainChute EZ will do the trick.

RAINCHUTE

RAINCHUTE EZ

LAWNSCAPE OUTLET

Gutters

Keep your gutters clean. There are a variety of gutter screening and cover materials that work well to keep them free of leaves and debris.

DON'T RELY ON CLEAN GUTTERS ALONE TO KEEP YOUR BASEMENT DRY.

CHAPTER SIX

THE SOLUTION, STEP 2
Isolate the House from the Earth

If your house has a dirt crawl space, you can't take your house out of the Earth, but you can keep the earth out of your house.

Now that groundwater is not an issue in your crawl space — either because you never had any, or because you've installed drainage and a sump pump to get rid of it — you're ready to deal with the water vapor (and the bugs) that arrive via the exposed earth.

This step is the key to solving your dirt crawl space problem. This is where you turn your nasty crawl space into a nice crawl space!

In deciding how to isolate your crawl space (and your house) from the earth, there are a few criteria you will need to meet. The solution must:

1. **Stop water vapor from flowing up from the soil**
2. **Stop water vapor from flowing through or off the crawl space walls**
3. **Allow water to drain from the walls to the sump location**
4. **Allow water to drain from the floor to the sump location**
5. **Not get ruined when someone crawls on it**
6. **Be durable so it lasts as long as the house does**
7. **Be affordable**

BONUS 8 – **Be treated with an antimicrobial ingredient so mold and bacteria will not grow on it**

There are two basic approaches: a concrete floor and a plastic liner.

Concrete Floors

If you pour concrete in your crawl space, you have accomplished two of our criteria: the concrete won't get ruined when someone crawls on it, and it will last. However, the concrete doesn't allow water from the walls or floor to drain to the sump location, and it doesn't stop water vapor from the walls or floor. In fact, water vapor goes right through concrete, especially a thin layer of concrete, such as might be installed in a crawl space.

You can solve these problems. To stop water vapor from the floor, you'll have to lay down a vapor barrier at least 6 mils thick before pouring the concrete. The vapor barrier stops the moisture, and the concrete makes it durable. But we also have to do something to let water flow under it. For that, we'll have to put down a layer of clean stone or gravel prior to laying our vapor barrier and pouring our concrete.

We also need to drain our walls. Crawl space walls are usually made of concrete block and they readily leak. We can put 6 mil plastic on the walls, but plastic is difficult to attach permanently to the walls and is not durable. One solution is to run the plastic from the floor up the walls and attach a wire mesh to the wall over the plastic. Then a stucco coat of concrete can be applied to the walls before the floor is poured.

Concrete is heavy, and mixing enough by yourself to cover your entire crawl space floor and walls is out of the question. To pour a floor 3 inches thick over a 1500-square-foot crawl space floor requires 14.4 cubic yards (or 30,000 pounds) of concrete. That is 1½ truckloads. Getting concrete from a truck into your crawl space is a whole different matter. You usually can't drag the heavy stuff to the back recesses of your crawl space in buckets fast enough before it hardens.

Getting a concrete pump is an option. The truck dumps concrete into a trailer-mounted pump, which pumps it through a hose into your crawl space, where workers can spread it out as best they can. I would caution that concrete is caustic and can cause severe burns.

Concrete?
Not the Solution

Concrete floors, unless combined with ways to drain the walls and floor, and ways to stop the water vapor from the walls and floor, are *not the answer.*

I have seen an unwary worker emerge from a crawl space where he was kneeling and sloshing around in wet concrete for a few hours trying to get the job done. He wound up with severe chemical burns on his legs, arms and sides.

Trying to figure out solutions to all the challenges of fixing a crawl space with concrete, one company tries to mix Portland cement with vermiculite to make it lighter. Concrete is usually made of Portland cement, sand, stone, and water.

The mixture of Portland cement and vermiculite, which may be best described to a layperson as "natural Styrofoam beads," makes for a weak final product — one you can feel your kneecaps sink into when you crawl on it. Some vermiculite, from a mine that has now been closed, contains asbestos.

When concrete is pumped into a crawl space, there is a strong urge to add extra water to the mix to make it flow more easily. This, however, weakens the concrete and makes it crack as it dries. Further, you have no chance of getting loose concrete to stay up on crawl space walls.

While you can make concrete work as a crawl space solution, the cost and challenges of preparing for it, and placing it, make it hard to argue that it's the best option. There is a better way.

Plastic Liners

In the past, it has been popular to lay down thin (such as 6 mil) plastic on crawl space floors. In fact, the building code has allowed an option to cut the venting requirement by 90% if 6 mil plastic is installed. But thin plastic does not meet our criteria that our solution must not get ruined when somebody crawls on it, and that it must last as long as the house does. Six mil polyethylene easily rips and gets holes poked in it when you crawl on it. Further, it is very difficult to attach to walls and can be easily pulled down.

Contractors and homeowners report that 6 mil poly has to be repaired all the time because of holes and rips that occur when they go into the crawl space. One said he had ripped holes in it with his belt buckle and cell phone antenna.

Can you believe that one contractor laid carpet remnants on top of the 6 mil poly to try to reduce the number of holes and tears?

How Many Times Is Enough?

One ideal I try to live by is this: if we want the house to last for over 100 years, then anything we put on it or in it to protect it should last as long. Otherwise, we'll have to do the same job again in the future. Thin polyethylene film doesn't cut it.

THIS HOME HAD a 6 mil polyethylene ground cover — but, because it had holes in it and wasn't sealed at the perimeter up the walls, and because the vents were left open, the house rotted anyway.

Extreme Makeover, Crawl Space Edition

I recommend a product called CleanSpace, which is made to perform to all the requirements listed at the beginning of this chapter. CleanSpace is a 20 mil thick plastic liner, similar to a pool liner, that can be fitted in your crawl space to completely seal off your home from the earth.

CleanSpace has multiple layers of plastics with different characteristics of flexibility and puncture and tear resistance. Put together with two layers of polyester cord reinforcement, the material is incredibly durable, will last as long as the house, and will stay where you install it. To make things even better, CleanSpace is bright white, which dramatically transforms your crawl space from the nasty pit it was to one you wouldn't hesitate to slide around in.

As an added benefit, CleanSpace has an antimicrobial additive manufactured into the material, which prevents mold growth on the liner. This additive is odorless and safe, and is used in many plastic household and automotive products.

To satisfy the criteria for our crawl space walls — stopping water vapor and allowing for drainage to the sump — we install CleanSpace, fastening it to the upper part of the walls. We stay 3 inches down from the top of the walls so that termites cannot get to the framing without their mud tunnels being seen. The CleanSpace liner is attached to the walls with fasteners along the top edge, which are permanently driven into the walls. Because of the crisscross layers of polyester cord reinforcements within the liner, you cannot pull it off of the walls or tear the CleanSpace around the fasteners.

With this method, we easily satisfy our requirements to allow drainage from the floor to the sump, and to stop water vapor from permeating up from the floor. When we lay the CleanSpace liner over the floor of the crawl space, water can seep or even flow under it to the sump, especially via any drainage channels we may have created before we installed it.

THE CLEANSPACE CRAWL SPACE ENCAPSULATION SYSTEM satisfies all of the repair criteria while dramatically transforming the area into healthy, usable space.

This crawl space has no more humidity than the space upstairs.

Crawl Spaces with Existing Concrete Floors

Crawl spaces with concrete floors can be treated in the exact same manner, by installing a sump at the lowest spot and then putting in a CleanSpace liner. One adaptation we can make is to lay down dimpled polyethylene drainage matting on the floor before installing the CleanSpace liner. This creates an air space through which water can flow over the concrete floor to the sump.

We have done many of these jobs, which illustrates that pouring a concrete floor in a crawl space is not the answer to the problem.

The liner is sealed around obstructions and at the seams by a variety of methods, including special tapes and sealants. The top edge around the walls is sealed with urethane caulk. If the CleanSpace liner is on a sloped dirt floor, the liner can be staked to the floor so it doesn't move or pull downward when you crawl on it.

Another benefit of this method and material is that you can use your crawl space for storage after installation — something homeowners could never consider in a dirt crawl space.

CleanSpace is manufactured specifically for this purpose. As such it has an antimicrobial agent called UltraFresh right in the plastic, which prevents mold and bacteria growth. It is used in other products, such as plastic automotive air ducts and seats, to prevent mold.

A DIMPLED POLYETHYLENE MEMBRANE under the CleanSpace liner allows water to flow to a sump in a crawl space that already has a concrete floor.

Provide for Plumbing Leaks in Your Crawl Space

A plumbing leak in a dirt crawl space will seep into the dirt forever (because you'll never notice it), keeping the dirt wet and the humidity up. When a CleanSpace system is installed, a plumbing leak can fill up your crawl space like a swimming pool. To prevent this, the sump systems described in Chapter 5, SmartSump and TripleSafe, have airtight lids with floor drains that drain water from the top of the CleanSpace liner in the event of a plumbing leak.

If you don't have groundwater leakage, you won't need a sump system in your crawl space. However, you still need to provide for plumbing leaks. You can do this with a SmartDrain.

A SmartDrain is a drywell-type unit that gets installed in your crawl space along with the CleanSpace liner. It features an alarm and an airtight floor drain in its lid. In the event of a plumbing leak, the alarm sounds, alerting you to the leak, and the water drains away into the soil under the CleanSpace until you get the leak fixed.

Radon Gas

Radon is a naturally occurring radioactive gas that comes from radium deposits in the earth's crust. If present in the soil under your home, it can get sucked into your house via the basement or crawl space.

Don't panic. It's fairly common and easy to get rid of.

CleanSpace is a passive radon reduction system all by itself. If an "active" system needs to be installed, a fan can draw air from below the CleanSpace and exhaust it outside above the highest eave. In this case, CleanSpace represents the majority of the work and expense to get rid of the radon (if you have it), so it shouldn't cost much to add a fan and exhaust pipe.

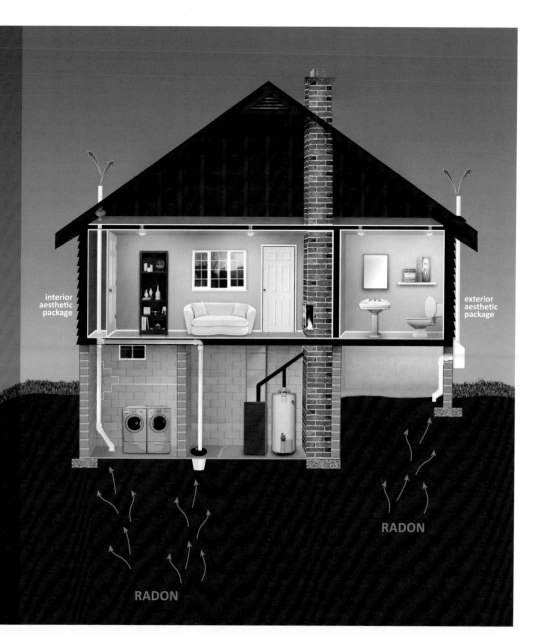

interior aesthetic package

exterior aesthetic package

RADON

RADON

CHAPTER SEVEN

THE SOLUTION, STEP 3
Seal Out "Evil" Outside Air

· ·

Air never rests. It is always in motion, and because of the "stack effect," it is constantly being drawn into your crawl space from the outside. Keeping it out is going to be a challenge, because air can slip through the tiniest of cracks. So let's get started...

BEFORE

AFTER

SEAL IT.
The CleanSpace vent covers seal the air out, insulate and improve the appearance.

Now that you don't have any moisture from the earth, you don't need vents — they only made the moisture problem worse and drained you of energy dollars every month. So let's seal them up!

Special CleanSpace vent covers from Basement Systems are designed to do the trick. They are plastic (so they won't rust or rot) and gasketed for an airtight seal using fasteners drilled into the wall.

This will make a HUGE improvement in your crawl space!

Your Crawl Space Access Door Should Seal Tight

A SNUG-FITTING all-plastic door stops air and moisture from entering.

Many crawl spaces have an access door to the outside. Most often it is made of plywood, and because it's down by the ground it rots easily. These rotted, warped doors usually seal poorly and look like heck.

The answer is an all-plastic door that won't rot, warp or need paint, and that bugs won't eat. Knobs screw into anchors in the wall to draw the door tight against weather stripping to seal off outside air. Perfect.

Once the liner is installed and the vents and air openings to the outside are closed, your crawl space will begin to dry out. **There is just one step left: dehumidification.**

Seal All Air Leaks to the Outside

When a CleanSpace system is installed, you want to seal vents to keep out unconditioned outside air. But vents aren't the only way outside air can get into your crawl space. Spaces under the sill plate and around pipes and wires to the outside, poorly fitting or rotted hatch doors, and other odd openings are all paths that need to be sealed to get the best results.

One area that was previously ignored is the open cavities at the top of block walls. Block walls are most common in dirt crawl spaces. Outside air goes right through porous block walls, then travels up and out the top of the wall into the crawl space.

To seal the top of the block walls, we developed a product called CleanSpace WallCap, an L-shaped molding that slips right on top of the block wall and covers the space the sill plate does not. Because it's made of clear plastic, it doesn't have to be removed for termite inspections.

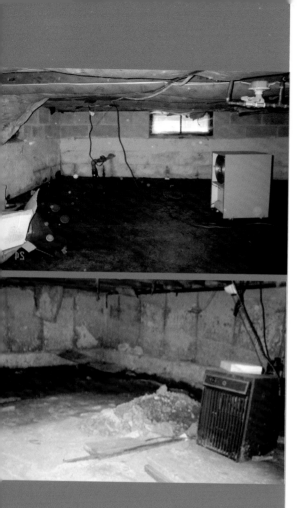

Didn't have a chance.

Running a dehumidifier in a vented and/or dirt crawl space is pointless. You can never dehumidify a space that has exposed earth, water or outside air leaking into it.

Keep Outside Air Out

Once the vents are sealed, then all other sources of outside air leakage into the crawl space need to be sealed. You may have a space between the sill plate and the top of the foundation. You may have openings around wires and pipes to the outside. You may have spaces or holes open to the garage, where unconditioned outside air is entering the crawl space. All these openings need to be sealed with caulk, flashing, spray foam or whatever material necessary.

STOP THE OUTSIDE AIR. Seal all openings where outside air can get into your crawl space, such as along the sill plate, and around pipes and wires to the outside.

When Your Crawl Space Access Is Below Grade

If your crawl space entrance is below the ground outside, it likely lets in air and collects water and debris. Typically, access wells are rotted and leaky — features that we're trying to avoid in our mission to control the crawl space environment. They are often too small, rusty or rotted, and hazardous (because people can fall into them). Aside from that — they're ugly!

The Turtl access well addresses these issues by combining a secure crawl space door and access well that has no leaky joints. Since it is made from rigid plastic, the Turtl will never rot or corrode—and as an added benefit, it's secure and lockable. It's also a lot more attractive than that old access well.

The Turtl access well — it's clean and dry, secure and lockable, and looks great from the outside. Made for a healthy crawl space.

Sights like these are a thing of the past. Old, leaky crawl space access systems can damage your home and present safety hazards.

VARIETY! The Turtl comes in three attractive colors.

You are on your way to a dry, energy-efficient crawl space – and a home that is less expensive, more comfortable, and healthier to live in!

CHAPTER EIGHT

THE SOLUTION, STEP 4
Keep Your Crawl Space Air Dry

Even the most thorough job of sealing out the outside air may leave your space feeling humid. You may still see some condensation in the hot days of summer. Our job here is not yet done...

Mastering Humidity: The Anti-Mold

Even though we have sealed off the earth and sealed air leaks to the outside, we will still have some air infiltration. Our crawl space sucks air in through the tiniest of spaces. And since our crawl space is cool in summer relative to the incoming air, we are cooling that air, and raising its relative humidity, once it enters. There are a few solutions; the best one is dehumidification.

Not so easy to do unless you have the right equipment. It just so happens that we do...

In order to eliminate condensation you need to either heat the air (ridiculous in summer) or take water out of it, which is easy to do. Correction. It is not so easy to take water out of the air *efficiently and effectively* unless you have the right equipment.

Not Just Any Dehumidifier

A dehumidifier is the plain answer. But not just any dehumidifier. I have been dealing with this issue intensely for nearly twenty years. The only machine that will get you the results you need is one called a SaniDry Crawl Space Air System. It's awesome.

The SaniDry is a high-capacity, high-efficiency dehumidification system, with air filtration, in a single unit. The SaniDry takes up to 100 pints of water per day out of your crawl space air, while using the same energy as a 40 pint dehumidifier. And it filters particles out of the air to less than an incredible 2 microns in size — smaller than any mold spore or dust mite dropping. The SaniDry air system wrings your air dry, and its powerful blower moves that dry air into and around your crawl space. This dry air then dries your building materials and contents, which makes the damp smell and damp feeling go away. This makes a huge difference during condensation season, summer. People really love their dry crawl spaces after having a SaniDry installed.

SANIDRY SEDONA The SaniDry Sedona air system will dry any basement or crawl space — no matter how damp — and keep it that way.

NOT JUST ON CONCRETE.
Condensation can form on cold water pipes and ducts, too.

The SaniDry Sedona crawl space air system wrings your air dry, and its powerful blower moves that dry air out into and around your crawl space. This dry air then dries your building materials and crawl space contents, which makes the damp smell and damp feeling go away! What a huge difference a SaniDry Sedona can make in "condensation season." People really love their dry crawl space environments after having a SaniDry Sedona installed.

You'll also never have to empty any buckets with your SaniDry Sedona because it automatically drains into your WaterGuard system or sump.

Having a groundwater-free crawl space is one thing. Adding a SaniDry Sedona is like placing the cherry on top of your dry crawl space program. It makes it complete. All below grade spaces need one.

The SaniDry Sedona is Energy Star rated — a rare achievement for a dehumidification system. Not only that, it is the most efficient dehumidifier in the world!*

Another big benefit of the SaniDry Sedona air system is that it doesn't have to be in the space it's drying. You can locate it in a utility room and duct the wet air in and dry air out to the main room of your crawl space.

With no water leaks and dry air, materials stay dry and you can use your crawl space for storage. No smell, no mold, no property damage.

*Without a bulky heat exchange core which doubles its size and makes a lot of noise.

Why Household Dehumidifiers Just Don't Do the Job

1. The unit is too small.

2. The cold coil (the actual thing that takes the water out of the air) **is too small.**

3. The fan is too small (it has to be so it doesn't blow the air past the dinky coil too fast, otherwise it wouldn't take any water out!)

4. The fan doesn't circulate the dry air around your crawl space — because it's too small.

5. They usually aren't drained automatically, so the bucket fills up and they shut off.

6. They are rated to remove only 25 pints, 30 pints, 40 pints, etc. per day at 80°F air temperature. Warm air holds a lot more moisture than cold air. Put them in a 68°F crawl space and their effectiveness goes way down below this number.

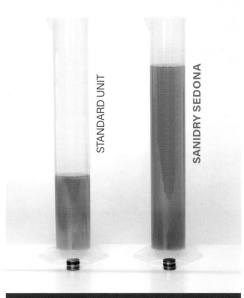

Water (colored for visibility) removed by standard household dehumidifier vs. SaniDry Sedona **for same electricity cost.**

There is simply no comparison between a SaniDry Sedona and any dehumidifier you've ever seen. I am usually a bit conservative and always realistic about what a product can do. The SaniDry Sedona is one product where I let all the performance promises hang out.

Open Sump Hole?

Having an open sump hole and running a dehumidifier is like trying to fill a bucket with a hole in it. As you dry the air, more water evaporates into it via the open sump hole with a pool of water sitting in it all year. In other words, you have a dehumidifier and a humidifier.

Dehumidifiers Should Drain Automatically

Quick: How many hours in a week? **168.**

How long would it take a cheapo dehumidifier's bucket to fill up and shut off? **Maybe 12.**

If you empty it once a week, what percentage of the time is it actually running? **If you're not a mathlete, the answer is 7% of the time. Meaning it's off 93% of the time.**

Who wants to have "Empty dehumidifier bucket" on their daily chore sheet? The answer is to **hook it up with a hose to drain the water away automatically** — and you never have to empty it.

Question: What Makes a Crawl Space Smell Like One?
Answer: Mold

Mold can grow in a waterproofed crawl space.

Mold needs organic material to grow (which you have), and high relative humidity — over 60% to 70%. It doesn't have to be wet for mold to grow, just humid. In fact, mold won't grow underwater.

A SaniDry Sedona ensures that the relative humidity stays below 55% all year long.

There are a lot of mold experts. One who tells you to eliminate the mold without eliminating the water and humidity is not helping you. Some tell you to coat your floor joists and other structural elements with anti-mold paint.

This implies that if it's humid and mold wants to grow, the paint will stop it from growing. Assuming that's true, what about the contents of your crawl space? If you have a cardboard box, does it have to be painted, too? How about your sofa? Call me crazy, but if it's really dry down there with low humidity, mold won't grow with or without a coating.

(I'm not crazy; that's the way it works.)

Dry, Clean Air – The Ultimate Purifier

Air is a very small thing. It gets in, around and between all your contents and building materials – into the smallest places. If that air has been dried by a SaniDry Sedona, it picks up moisture from these contents (dries them) and goes through the Sedona to be dried again – and out to the space to dry your contents once more. Dry air dries things, and mold doesn't stand a chance on dry things.

Save Money
Dry Air Is Easier to Cool!

Damp indoor air costs more money to cool. Sure, there's a small cost to running a SaniDry Sedona, but lower cooling costs partly offset this electricity cost. This is because your central air system has to remove the moisture from the air in order to cool it, and that takes energy. Air conditioning systems are inefficient at dehumidifying.

If you dry the air in your crawl space, that air rises into the rest of the house, making the whole house drier. You'll also feel more comfortable at a higher temperature with less humidity in the whole house.

SaniDry Sedona – Energy Test Winner!

We tested four dehumidifiers to find out the cost per pint of water removed from the air. The worst performer was a standard household unit available under any number of recognizable brand names. It came out at more than 11 cents per pint removed. A higher priced unit, but without the features of the SaniDry Sedona, cost about 10 cents per pint of water removed. The big winner was the SaniDry Sedona, which cost only 3.3 cents per pint of water removed! What a bargain!

Dust Mites
#1 INDOOR ALLERGEN

The No. 1 thing that people with asthma and allergies react to indoors is dust mite droppings. Dust mites live in your furniture, bedding, and carpeting, and feed off dead skin flakes. Their droppings are so small that they become airborne, are breathed in, and thus can irritate humans. Dust mites need relative humidity above 50% to live, as they absorb water out of the air rather than drinking it. Therefore, dry the air and dust mites die.

We have heard of a doctor in West Virginia who prescribed a SaniDry unit on his prescription pad! Now there's an enlightened doctor!

For more information go to **www. housedustmite.org.**

How does it perform so incredibly well with the same amount of energy that less-effective 20-pound-weakling dehumidifiers use?

1. Designed to perform in lower air temperatures found in crawl spaces and basements.

2. Larger, higher performace components (compressor, condenser and evaporator coils)

3. Processes (filters and dries) 300 cubic feet of your basement air per minute compared to about 50 cfm for other models.

POWERFUL BLOWER. The blower really moves dehumidified air around to dry the entire space.

Did I mention I love the SaniDry Sedona? I know you will, too.

Floor Insulation: Now You Need It, Now You Don't

After a CleanSpace installation, you do not need insulation in the floor. So if the insulation is moldy or in bad shape, you can remove it and not worry about replacing it. By closing vents, sealing other air leaks, and installing CleanSpace, you are making a world of difference in your home's energy efficiency. If you want to take a next incremental step, a radiant barrier could be installed on the crawl space walls, or those walls can be insulated with foam — methods that we'll address on the following pages (read on).

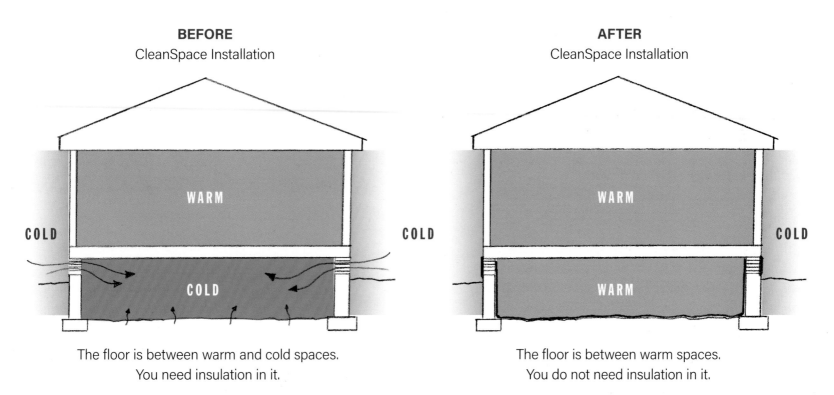

BEFORE
CleanSpace Installation

AFTER
CleanSpace Installation

The floor is between warm and cold spaces. You need insulation in it.

The floor is between warm spaces. You do not need insulation in it.

Adding Insulation

By isolating the house from the earth and sealing air leaks from the outside, you will have made a huge leap forward in the energy efficiency of your home.

To Crawl Space Walls

If you want to take incremental steps to save as much energy as possible, have foam insulation boards installed on your crawl space walls. SilverGlo paneling has tiny graphite particles in its foam insulation to give it that silver/gray shine. These tiny particles reflect heat and lower the material's conductivity for superior R value per inch. In addition to resisting heat conduction, SilverGlo boasts a radiant barrier, which reflects heat back into your crawl space for ultimate energy savings.

To the Crawl Space Floor

You can also insulate your crawl space floor (which can be as cool as 55°) under the CleanSpace with TerraBlock. TerraBlock is ¾ inch thick flexible foam insulation with a vapor barier on both sides. It adds R value, puncture resistance, and dreamy padding for your knees. TerraBlock is for those who want to save the most on their energy costs.

Using SilverGlo to insulate your rim joist (the perimeter of your floor system) makes a lot of sense too!

Duct Leakage

First Your Enemy, Now Your Friend
(Skip if you have hot water heat.)

As we said, when you have a vented dirt crawl space, duct leakage serves to distribute damp, moldy air throughout the house, as well as distributing some of your energy dollars out the window (or rather, out the vents).

After the vents to the outside are sealed and a CleanSpace system is installed, however, duct leakage, which could be 300 cubic feet of air per minute, is your friend.

Why? Because it distributes conditioned (heated, cooled, dried) air from your HVAC system into and out of your crawl space. This dries your crawl space. And since there is no way for the air to get out of the crawl space to the exterior, it only serves to help the upstairs environment, too. For example, heat leaking out of a supply duct will rise and warm and dry the floors above. The first floor will be cheaper to heat because its floor will be warm instead of cold.

Duct leakage is also an accidental way to get combustion air into a crawl space. Just make sure that there are no big holes in the return ducts.

Dryer Vents — as Evil as Air Comes

Never vent a dryer into a crawl space. All that water from your skivvies will cause a big moisture problem in your crawl space — no matter what season it is. Duct dryer vents outside.

A DRYER VENT ONLY ADDS to the moisture load in your crawl space.

Combustion Appliances

If you have a furnace or water heater in your crawl space that requires air for combustion of gas or oil, you may need to allow air to enter the crawl space for that purpose. This air, once used to burn fuel, goes up the chimney. The idea is, if you create a vacuum in your crawl space because you sealed it up so tight, then you will not have a draft to take exhaust gases up the chimney from your furnace or water heater.

We are talking about appliances that are atmospherically vented — meaning that they take in air for combustion from the room they are in. Your water heater and gas furnace unit are most likely atmospherically vented, unless they are newer, high-efficiency, units.

When I think about the thousands of basements I have been in, even small ones, which almost always have combustion appliances in them, I can probably count on one hand the times I have seen fresh combustion air brought in for them. They draw in air from inside the building to burn and exhaust up the chimney. There is enough air leakage in a basement, even without vents, that adequate combustion air is not a problem.

"Normal air infiltration" in a building is considered adequate by the building code for combustion air supply. However, a crawl space is smaller than a basement, and you are sealing it up tight as part of your strategy to stop moisture. If there are combustion appliances located in the crawl space, there has to be a way for them to get air to maintain proper draft all of the time.

You must not depressurize a space where combustion appliances are located.

One easy way to provide combustion air is to install two vents in the crawl space ceiling to the first floor. This way air can be drawn down into the crawl space if the combustion appliances need it. It's better than the alternative, which is to leave a vent to the outside open, allowing "evil" unconditioned (hot, cold, wet) outside air to enter. The International Residential Code (2000) allows for the installation of vents to adjoining indoor spaces for combustion air.

A combustion air supply unit is a good option. A "fan-in-a-can" is a fan wired to your burner circuit. When the burner turns on, the fan blows in air for combustion.

For new homes, or when replacing your water heater or HVAC unit, you should use high-efficiency direct-vent appliances, instead of atmospherically vented ones. Direct-vent appliances have an inlet where you attach a dedicated combustion air supply duct from the outside. This satisfies the whole combustion air supply issue, and you'll never have to worry about where or how to vent in combustion air.

It is important to have a carbon monoxide (CO) alarm if you have combustion appliances or attached garages.

Fixing Your Crawl Space Pays for Itself

On one hand, one could argue that the net cost to fix a crawl space is zero, since you will save money each month in energy costs and avoid costly rot and mold repairs. In fact, you could say that fixing a dirt crawl space actually pays, since you will eventually save more than it costs.

Nevertheless, there is an investment up front to have the work done, and the savings accrue over the years. There are variables to consider. The area of your crawl space, the height of your crawl space, how much drainage work you may or may not need, the sump, the battery-powered backup pump, and dehumidification are all factors that will affect what you can expect to pay. A complete system in a large home could cost much more.

One thing is for sure. You can't justify what you paid for your home and then say it's okay to let the conditions in your crawl space fester and threaten your investment.

CleanSpace is one of those things that you are going to pay for whether you get it or not. This makes it a no-brainer to get it!

Save 15% to 25% on Energy Costs

An independent study revealed that homeowners who properly fix their vented dirt crawl space can save 15% to 25% on their heating and air conditioning costs!

FIXING YOUR CRAWL SPACE properly is probably the smartest and most financially rewarding home repair you'll ever make.

Crawl Space No-No's

Don't put a vapor barrier or rigid insulation board on the ceiling of your crawl space (unless your home is on stilts).

- Don't close vents without sealing the earth.
- Don't seal the earth without closing the vents.
- Never use a fan to blow outside air into your crawl space.
- Never use a fan to blow air out of your crawl space.
- Don't install a liner or concrete without removing organic material such as wood, cardboard, insulation, etc., from the dirt floor first.
- Don't depressurize a space that has combustion appliances (more than 1 pascal).
- Don't run your dryer vent into your crawl space.
- Don't ignore the problem.

A VAPOR BARRIER on the bottom of floor joists traps water above it to rot the lumber.

POWER FANS like this can make your mold, moisture, rot and energy problems worse — fast!

RIGID INSULATION BOARD on the crawl space ceiling creates a moisture pocket against the floor joists.

CHAPTER NINE

LIES THE BUILDING CODE TOLD ME

Time for a Change in Crawl Space Standards

What do you do when regulations and bureaucracy lag behind the proven science? First, you stick to the science and fix what needs to be fixed. You fix it the right way, whether or not the right way is officially sanctioned. And while you're at it, you make some noise. You call for the code to catch up with the research.

The building code allows dirt crawl spaces that are vented. In fact, it requires them to be vented. Recently, in the 2000 International Residential Code, they have added exceptions to the venting provision (which don't make complete sense to me).

One exception says, "Where warranted by climatic conditions, ventilation openings to the outdoors are not required if ventilation openings to the interior are provided." So you can have a dirt crawl space and vent it to the inside of your home? And what climatic conditions are they talking about anyway?

At least these exceptions give us a hint that some of the people who write the code know that something isn't right.

Don't get me wrong; homes in the United States today are safer than those in many other countries because of our building code. That's great. The building code protects us. But on the crawl space issue, the code has been so wrong for so many years. Twenty years ago we could chalk it up to ignorance. But now we know what the problem is. How long can it be before someone points to the building code and says, "This rotted my house" or "This is responsible for the mold in my house"?

All truth passes through three stages.

FIRST, it is *ridiculed*.

SECOND, it is violently *opposed*.

THIRD, it is accepted as *self-evident*.

–Schopenhauer

There is a document from the Department of Energy that says "vented dirt crawl spaces are wrong" and to "close the vents." It goes on to say that they recognize that this is against the building code, so you might have to pull some creative explanation to get by the local inspector. Try calling your crawl space a "short basement," the Feds say, so the locals will allow it. It's really ridiculous.

So what should the code writers do? In my opinion, they should act now and change the code to disallow exposed earth under a house and forbid venting crawl spaces. They should admit their error in light of new research and get it over with. It's inevitable, so why wait any longer?

In some states, Arkansas for one, a division of the Department of Agriculture is somehow ordained with the job of moisture control in crawl spaces. Why? As near as I can tell, pest control operators, such as termite contractors, go into crawl spaces all the time and do "moisture control work" under homes. Since they use pesticides, which are regulated by the Department of Agriculture, then the same department got the regulation of moisture control.

These boards insist on ventilation. And if there is mold or rot, their solution is to add more vents. It has never worked. These boards must look at the results and compare it against evidence that supports ventilation (of which there is none), and change their codes accordingly. Inclusion in a code is not evidence that a practice works, no matter how old the code is!

One thing we have heard in the field is that some termite contractors won't warrant the house against termites if there is a liner in the crawl space. They say that they can't see the termites if they are there. This is just plain resistance to change and fear of what they don't understand. However, many are changing their mind on this issue.

A dry house is less likely to be eaten by termites. When we seal a crawl space, we leave a 3-inch strip of foundation wall exposed at the top so that pest control experts can inspect for termites anyway. Besides, what would they do if the crawl space had a concrete floor in it? What would they do if it were a basement? How about a finished basement where you can't see the floor or walls?

Are we to say that you cannot finish your basement because the termite guy can't see the walls and floor? And what if you can't get the necessary termite warranty on your house? Your bank won't let you close on the mortgage, so you can't buy the house or refinance? This is ridiculous.

What termite contractors should fear is that all of their customers with moldy crawl spaces will come back to them and say that, on the contractors' recommendation, they added vents that caused their houses to rot. Until now, you could rightly chalk this disaster up to old codes and ignorance. Now the new research is out and it's time for a change.

One of our dealers in South Carolina installed a CleanSpace system and sealed the vents in a home, which was then inspected by a home inspector before the house was sold. The home inspector told the buyer that the crawl space was illegally sealed up, and that it would surely rot unless it was put back the way it was. He really went on about how bad it was.

So our dealer hired Craig DeWitt, PhD, an engineer who specializes in moisture and energy issues, to come in and do an assessment.

Craig measured the relative humidity and wood moisture content and found them to be far lower (better) than the average conditions seen in vented dirt crawl spaces in the area. He issued a report saying that "the crawl space in its current configuration, is providing a durable, high-performance foundation system…. that will outperform a vented crawl space."

In all fairness to industry professionals, they are just going by what they've always done.

We all learn things from other people, and these professionals have accepted the "old way" as it was taught to them without doing any research and without making the observation that it is not working. Some termite contractors, code officials and building inspectors are on the leading edge of this issue, although they are in the minority as of this writing. The rest need to be enlightened. The good news is that it's simple and it doesn't hurt.

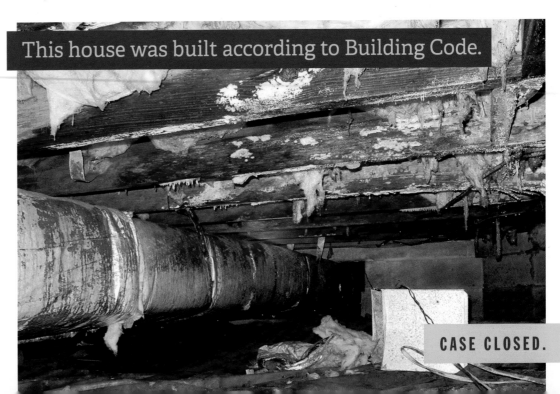

This house was built according to Building Code.

CASE CLOSED.

CHAPTER TEN

CRAWL SPACE REPAIR PROJECTS

Heaven and Hell

. . . .

Imagine that you were able to transform a moldy hole beneath your home into a clean, functional, bright, dry space that increased resale value and enhanced the health of everyone in your family. Guess what? You can do exactly that. Let the pictures tell the tale...

Take care of the leakage/drainage problem, isolate the house from the earth, close all outside air leaks, and you'll save money each month. You'll make your house a healthier, more comfortable place to live.

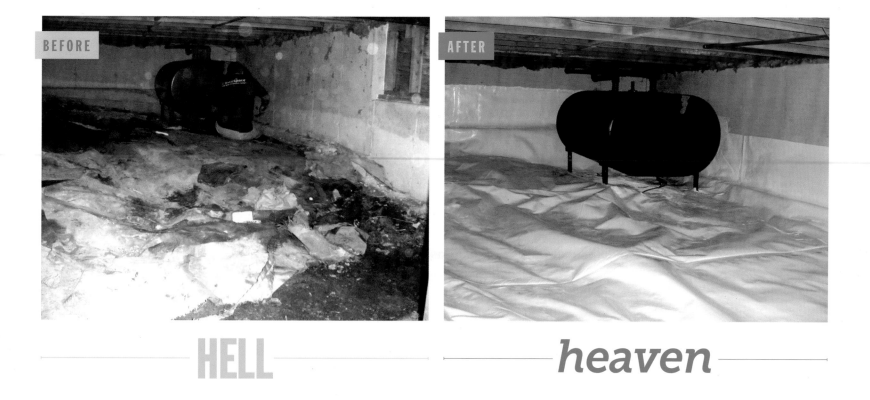

BEFORE

AFTER

HELL *heaven*

All these homeowners were extremely happy that they took action. Now they are experiencing energy savings every month. These are all photos of the CleanSpace Crawl Space Encapsulation System.

CleanSpace® *heaven*

CleanSpace® *heaven*

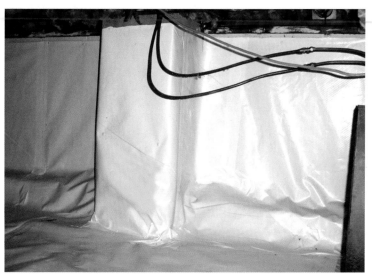

THESE HOMES will last decades longer with the CleanSpace system.

AFTER

CHAPTER ELEVEN

THE PERFECT CRAWL SPACE UNDERFOOT

If Money's No Object, Then Do This

Here it is. The gold standard. The complete package. Heaven on steroids. The most comprehensive solution available to address every aspect of your (formerly hellish) crawl space. Why settle for less?

Money is an object!

Okay, it is. But only if you expected to pay cash for this repair. Most people don't pay cash for an automobile, they finance it. There are all kinds of options to get your crawl space fixed right: a home equity loan, credit cards, or a home improvement loan, with which your dealer can help you.

If a house is worth the price you paid for it with a wet, damp, moldy lower level that causes property damage, rot, poor health, frustration and despair, then it is worth the price you paid plus $10,000 to own the same house with a dry, healthy crawl space. Make sense?

A vented dirt crawl space costs more money each year in heating and cooling bills and mold, rot and pest repairs. Our solution lowers some of these costs and eliminates others. Therefore . . . "You're going to pay for the repair whether you get it or not. So you may as well get it."

The Perfect Solution

- CleanSpace drainage matting on the floor with a CleanSpace encapsulation system with antimicrobial ingredient .... *see Chapter 6*

- A TripleSafe sump pump system with IceGuard (for crawl spaces with groundwater leakage, graded to sump location) or SmartDrain (for crawl spaces with no ground water leakage)....................... *see Chapter 5* and *Chapter 6*

- SaniDry air system .... *see Chapter 8*

- CleanSpace vent covers .... *see Chapter 7*

- EverLast crawl space door (if your door is leaky), WallCap (if you have open-topped block walls) and all other outside air leaks sealed................ *see Chapter 7*

The price will vary widely with how big the crawl space is, the amount of drainage work, vents, doors, sump equipment, etc. Consult your local Basement Systems dealer or CleanSpace installer for a written estimate and exact price in your home.

10% is a lot of money!

Because buyers view your home with a damp, moldy crawl space as a fixer-upper, they will pay you 10% less than otherwise—that's if they buy it at all. Using this formula...

Value of Your Home	The cost of not fixing your crawl space in property value alone
$100,000	$10,000
$150,000	$15,000
$200,000	$20,000
$300,000	$30,000
$400,000	$40,000
$500,000	$50,000
$600,000	$60,000

You get the idea. And this does not take into account the cost of mold remediation, rot repairs or higher energy bills each month while you live there!

The Moral of the Story

Fixing your crawl space is a lot cheaper than **NOT** fixing your crawl space!

Buyers Expect a Dry Crawl Space

Who wants to buy a home with a damp, moldy crawl space? Nobody! It's difficult enough to find a buyer who wants your house, and heartbreaking when they walk away after looking at the crawl space.

In most states, there are disclosure forms which ask the seller a range of questions about their knowledge of defects with the property. One of the questions asks if you ever had any mold in the home. In addition, most buyers hire home inspectors to inspect the property for defects. Home inspectors have a keen eye for moisture and mold problems because that's what they are hired for. There is simply no hiding your crawl space problem when you sell your home. And if you do disclose your crawl space problem, either nobody will buy, or they will make a low offer. In fact, buyers will discount the price of a home by 10% or more because of a damp, moldy crawl space.

FIX IT
TO
LIST IT

Remember, you are going to spend more if you don't fix it!

Now you've read the very latest, cutting-edge Crawl Space Science. You are an educated consumer and know what to have done to your home and why. Your local Basement Systems dealer can help you with the items discussed in this book because we know all of this stuff and live it every day. To find your local dealer, visit www.DirtCrawlSpace.com. Thank you!

Dealer Locations

WE'RE THERE.

The Basement Systems dealer network spans North America, the United Kingdom and Ireland.

CONTRACTOR
NATION

About the Author

Larry Janesky is an authority on basement and crawl space repair and building effective businesses that serve homeowners well. In 1982, at age 17, he began five years of self-employment as a carpenter and builder before founding Basement Systems, Inc. Today, Basement Systems is the largest network of waterproofing and crawl space repair contractors in the world. Larry has taken personal responsibility for repairing more than 50,000 basements and crawl spaces over 30 years through his local installation business in Connecticut. Larry is also president of Total Basement Finishing, a leading network of finishing contractors, and Dr. Energy Saver, a network of contractors that provide home comfort services. Larry has trained thousands of talented, dedicated basement repair contractors and their employees in the past 25 years. He holds 30 patents. Larry is the author of Dry Basement Science, Crawl Space Science, Basement Finishing Science, Saving Energy and Money at Home. He has also authored an award-winning novel, The Highest Calling: An Inspirational Novel About Business and Life, Struggle and Success. He writes a daily blog called "Think Daily," received by nearly 30,000 people each morning.

Larry enjoys seeing everyone around him succeed. His mission is to make the world a better place for homeowners, employees, and businesspeople by helping build successful businesses that serve all effectively.

He lives in Connecticut and enjoys outdoor activities with his family. Larry is a passionate motocross rider; in 2015 he and his son won the Baja 1000, the longest nonstop cross-country motorcycle race in the world.

Acknowledgments

Some may think that crawl spaces are unglamorous, uncelebrated and unimportant. Unglamorous and uncelebrated, yes. Unimportant, no! When it's what you do every day, and you can save homeowners billions of dollars every year, protecting assets and improving health for millions, it's very important. My vision is we stop building these energy-wasting nasty holes under our homes, and fix all 26 million of them out there.

I would like to acknowledge the following for their contributions.

- Mike Delmolino and Lou Bemer at Basement Systems CleanSpace Department.
- Joe Lstiburek and his Building Science Corp., www.buildingscience.com.
- Craig Dewitt at RLC Engineering, Clemson, SC, www.RLCengineering.com.
- Fine Homebuilding magazine, for publishing my article "Sealing Crawl Spaces" in their March 2003 issue, No. 153, www.finehomebuilding.com.
- Kevin Koval at Adirondack Basement Systems in Clifton Park, New York.
- Rod Martin at Complete Basement Systems of Denver, Colorado, and Pete Karreman at Omni Basement Systems, Toronto, for photos.
- Harold Shapiro, photographer, Branford, Connecticut.
- Jeff Nelson, Chad Achenbach, Greg Smith, Sam Bullock, Jason Wood, Charlene Bieber and many others at Connecticut Basement Systems, for photos.
- The staff at my company, Basement Systems, Inc., and our many dealers, who are helping to make the world a better place by fixing crawl spaces every day. www.BasementSystems.com.
- Dr. Energy Saver dealers, nationwide.

Trusted Partners

CleanSpace is one of five sister companies with expansive contractor networks. All companies are industry leaders in their respective fields. Each has developed an informational book, much like Crawl Space Science, about problems homeowners face and their options for solutions. Visit their websites and request a free copy of their books, compliments of our network.

BasementSystems.com

MyCleanSpace.com

TotalBasementFinishing.com

TreehouseInternetGroup.com

DrEnergySaver.com

MoreHouseFinance.com

AtticSystems.com

TheSOE.com

FoundationSupportworks.com

NationalRadonDefense.com

JunkLuggers.com

KlausRoofingSystems.com

GutterShutter.com

Notes